Being Human at Work

■ ■ ■

Also by Richard Strozzi-Heckler

The Anatony of Change: A Way to Move Through Life's Transitions

Holding the Center: Sanctuary in a Time of Confusion

In Search of the Warrior Spirit: Teaching Awareness Disciplines to the Green Berets

Aikido and the New Warrior (ed.)

Being Human at Work

Bringing Somatic Intelligence into Your Professional Life

■ ■ ■

Edited by Richard Strozzi-Heckler

North Atlantic Books
Berkeley, California

Published by
North Atlantic Books
P.O. Box 12327
Berkeley, California 94712

Cover design by Susan Quasha
Text design by Brad Greene
Printed in Canada

Being Human at Work: Bringing Somatic Intelligence into Your Professional Life is sponsored by the Society for the Study of Native Arts and Sciences, a non-profit educational corporation whose goals are to develop an educational and crosscultural perspective linking various scientific, social, and artistic fields; to nurture a holistic view of arts, sciences, humanities, and healing; and to publish and distribute literature on the relationship of mind, body, and nature.

North Atlantic Books' publications are available through most bookstores. For further information, call 800-337-2665 or visit our website at www.northatlanticbooks.com.

Substantial discounts on bulk quantities are available to corporations, professional associations, and other organizations. For details and discount information, contact our special sales department.

Library of Congress Cataloging-in-Publication Data

Being human at work : bringing somatic intelligence into your professional life / edited by Richard Strozzi-Heckler.
    p. cm.
    ISBN 1-55643-447-2 (pbk.)
    1. Job satisfaction. 2. Mind and body. 3. Centering (Psychology)
    4. Motivation (Psychology) 5. Self-care, Health. 6. Job enrichment. I. Strozzi-Heckler, Richard.
    HF5549.5.J63B43 2004
    650.1'3--dc21

2003007621
CIP

1 2 3 4 5 6 7 8 9 TRANS 08 07 07 06 05 04 03

To Jack, Paloma, and Wesley

~

Acknowledgments

This book would not be what it is without the tireless effort, care, attention to detail, and loving management skills of Jean Dunham. Jean was always the lighthouse when the storms hit. Lindy Hough's vast editorial skills smoothed the rough edges and cut the fat; Sharron Wood's line editing brought everything up a notch. Forever grateful to Ariana, Jack, Paloma, Wesley, Django and Tiphani for their patience and goodwill in my life and in this project. Mark, Alice, and Gail at Strozzi Institute for their steadiness and commitment and for the many others who are too numerous to mention that have enriched my life and made this work possible. Thank you to all.

ᔧ Table of Contents

$\sim$ Introduction

We begin the twenty-first century dominated by a technological culture that, with remarkably few exceptions, has created social and economic institutions that treat people as instrumental means. Many of us live lives of ease and luxury, yet fewer and fewer of us can claim that what we are doing produces satisfaction. Even fewer seem able to answer with any depth the question: "What am I working so hard for?" The significant loss of productivity, innovation, and creativity at the workplace, not to mention the overwhelming despair that so many experience as a result of spending more than a third of their life in an activity that has little or no personal meaning, is a staggering cost to the human spirit.

This alienation and fragmentation in modern life—as evidenced by the billion dollar industries created by antidepressants, antacids, anxiety relievers, migraine medications, and flights to virtual worlds—suggests an inability to cope with the pressures of our personal and professional lives. The greatest cost of the specialization of technological life—and out of which all other damages are birthed—is arguably our separation from the practical and enriching sense of ourselves as embodied beings. When we are alienated from the wisdom of the body, our lives become theoretical and abstract, and we are distanced from the direct, felt sense of living. Our bodies become anxious, easily depressed, incapable of satisfaction, often ineffective, and victim to the purveyors of cosmetics, medicine, and the illusion of perpetual youth. Except as delivery mechanisms that haul

1

our brains from meeting to meeting, from work to home and back again, our bodies have grown inconsequential. Even at the gym our efforts to trim our bodies are mechanical and joyless. We have become afflicted by a cultural amnesia and have forgotten that we are feeling, multidimensional beings, rather than extras in some corporate extravaganza.

For the past eighteen years at the Strozzi Institute, The Center for Leadership and Mastery, we have investigated, researched and promoted a cogent and viable alternative to what ails us. It is a set of practices that allows the wisdom of our embodied humanity to lead the way. This doesn't mean, however, that productivity takes a back seat. Our research has shown that by empowering the individual with the skills of awareness, choice, commitment, and purposeful living, productivity and creativity increase.

The essays in this anthology speak of "somatics." "Somatics" is a Greek word that literally means "the living body in its wholeness." It refers to the notion that humans have the capacity to be self-generating, self-healing, and self-educating. Our work at Strozzi Institute is strongly influenced by the discipline of somatics, as well as linguistics, martial arts, philosophy, neurobiology, body-oriented psychology, and meditation. Somatics is a set of practices that produces:

- A centered presence in which we learn to be present to others while staying firmly grounded in what we care about
- The capacity to generate, receive, and repair trust when we break it
- Empathy and respect for others
- The ability to listen
- The knowledge of what it is to be authentic
- The ability to coordinate effectively with others
- The desire to be life-long learners.

All the authors in this anthology have studied at the Institute (the one exception, Richard Leider, is a long time friend and collaborator who has taught at Strozzi Institute) and have integrated this somatic work into their professional disciplines.

Richard Leider, a well-known author and consultant who has spent his entire career of more than thirty years studying purpose and calling, sets the tone for the book in the *Career as Calling* section when he asks, "Why do we do what we do?" Leider argues that purpose is essential to our fulfillment in the workplace; without it we drift aimlessly. First, Leider says, we need to respond to our natural desire to live a life of meaning and satisfaction.

In the "Leading the Way" section, I describe a learning environment within organizations that develops the self as the fundamental source of power for leaders. I propose that the self is indistinguishable from the body, and that training the body teaches the leadership skills necessary to build effective teams and trust among customers and colleagues.

Judith Rosenberg has been training leaders in low-income neighborhoods throughout the United States and Latin America to build sustainable, self-generating communities for almost two decades. Her work opens social implications in leadership training for people of color and the economically disadvantaged.

Ariana Strozzi uses horses to create an innovative approach to building leadership skills with individuals and teams. In her essay she shares lessons learned about leadership when her clients interact with horses.

Robert Dunham, a former executive at Motorola who heads his own consulting company, demonstrates how his method of teaching management skills allows people to make new behavioral choices, instead of simply memorizing a set of management tips and techniques. Dunham argues that most MBA graduates are head smart but ineffective when dealing with people.

Woody Allen (not the actor as he is fond of saying), a life-long athlete, has served as CEO, CFO, and chairman of a number of successful companies. He challenges us to adopt from sports training an ongoing set of practices to create more positive esprit in the workplace.

Tom Lutes offers a compelling account of the challenges and joys of working with mood and emotion in the blue-collar population of a large midwestern utilities company. We follow him as he transforms a resigned, disgruntled veteran of the production line into a self-reflective individual who embarks on a new way of life.

Peter Luzmore, a Brit by birth, has a long-standing belief that people don't have to suffer at work to be productive and successful. He demonstrates how somatic practices can increase both productivity and joy in the workplace, teaching his clients that synchronizing in movement improves their business … and fun.

Executive coach and trainer *Suzanne Zeman* proposes a way of working somatically over the phone to create trust, connection, and a mood of learning. Her work belies our assumptions regarding how we engage electronically with others.

New York state educator *Peter Reilly* proposes a radical model for training teachers to contact and listen to their students more effectively. Examples from decades of teaching and observing the needs of his students illustrate that the way we teach can be as important as *what* we teach.

Mary Wagner, prize-winning writer and teacher at San Francisco State University, describes the use of a somatic sensibility in helping young writers find their voice. To be a writer, she says, one must live with one's senses wide open. She shows how bringing aspiring writers into their bodies improves their craft and feeds their poetic imagination.

Peter Denning, a godfather of the computing industry, claims that engineering departments have failed in teaching their students how to produce value in the marketplace. Denning has produced a curriculum for engineering students that teaches them how to listen deeply to the concerns of their customers.

Karen Short, mother, parent educator, and consultant to schools, proposes that we've strayed from a fundamental common sense in how we relate to our children. She says that by learning the art of listening through our bodies we will have more satisfying relationships with our children, and they will learn more quickly.

Physician, poet, and hospice teacher *Patrick Clary* offers a new perspective for physicians working with death and dying. Clary describes his personal struggle confronting death in the jungles of Vietnam, during the Twin Towers tragedy, and with his individual clients. His is a moving account of a pioneer in the relatively new field of death and dying.

Psychotherapist and teacher *Denise Benson* describes the challenges of including the body when working with adolescents. She shows how she skillfully introduced a teenage client to a somatic understanding of her body, increasing her confidence, self-esteem, and capacity for self-expression.

Rich Poccia, an accomplished martial artist and health professional, proposes that martial arts are a rich context to help those with addictions. This unconventional wisdom challenges both our notions about the martial arts and our ideas of how to approach those who are in treatment for addictive behaviors.

In her work with couples *Paula Love* uses movement and gesture to help her clients develop more effective communication. Working through the body they learn practices they can use when the relationship begins to wobble.

Boston psychotherapist and coach *Jennifer Cohen* demonstrates how trauma stays alive in the body. By paying attention to habituated reactions, her clients learn to integrate the fragmented parts of themselves more easily.

J. Clare Bowen-Davies, another psychotherapist and coach, shows how working with the body in alcohol recovery allows healing to be deeper and more consistent. She argues that a somatic element should become standard practice in recovery work. In her case study we see how she counsels clients to experience the value of somatic practices.

Jan Mundo has created a hands-on method of healing headaches that may revolutionize the migraine industry. Her effective method of banishing headache pain also teaches her clients (physicians, nurses, health practitioners, and individuals) how they can work on themselves to ease their own pain.

Psychotherapist and coach *Michael Moran* illustrates the subtlety and long-lasting effect of working through the body. He posits that a somatic approach is essential in producing deep and lasting change.

Marine Captain John Duvall writes about his experience in the Marine Warrior Project, the prototype for the present version, called the Marine Martial Art. He speaks candidly about the value of facing fears for those in the military, and regards body/mind practices as fundamental for the training of the Marine of the twenty-first century.

Special Forces officer *Lieutenant Colonel Fred Krawchuk* describes a holistic approach to decision making as the military is confronted with new kinds of missions. Military leaders must now move quickly between "operations other than war" and a fast-changing battlefield, necessitating skills in new body/mind practices.

You don't have to read from the beginning to the end of this anthology. Pick out what interests you and expand from there. Our aim is not to introduce tips and techniques but to create a sensibility in which you begin to see yourself and the world anew. This sensibility is rooted in the fundamental virtues of self-reflection, respect for life, commitment to action, the primacy of relationship, and a collective vision for living a properly human life. Appreciating and engaging these issues invites us into the art of being human.

Richard Strozzi-Heckler, Ph.D.
Strozzi Institute
Petaluma, California

Part One

Career as Calling

Chapter 1

For the Sake of What?

∼ Richard Leider

Purpose. A hard word to define, perhaps, yet we're born with it. It may not have a name or a face. We may not see it as purpose, but it is there.

Purpose is the eternal quest to be connected with something larger than our own life. It is an answer to the spiritual question, "For the sake of what?"" For the sake of what am I living? What is the true meaning of my existence here and now? The word "purpose," misused and open to challenge as it is, still conveys a question that each of us must answer.

Purpose is like art. We know it when we embody it. It comes through us as we gaze at the northern lights in the clear, cold fall sky. It is the deep center we feel as we warm ourselves around a fire on the plains of East Africa. It is the helper's high we feel when we make a difference in another's life. We sense our place in the grand pattern of life. We feel centered.

Some people claim that there is no grand pattern of life, no reason for our being here. They claim that purpose is an invention of people who refuse to face the harsh realities of life or who deny death. They argue for purely rational explanations of our true nature.

We should not argue with these people. They are the people the Chinese philosopher Chuang Tzu observed when he wrote, "A frog in a well cannot be talked to about the sea."

If you sense a call to the sea—a purpose in your life—it's time to choose. You must leave the well to those who enjoy debating the temperature of the water in the well in which they are trapped. Their well is a place that they have chosen over a sea that is not yet seen.

Purpose is a path to the sea. There are many paths and, like life, paths are uncertain. Tennessee Williams wrote, "There is a time of departure even when there's no certain place to go." How do we know when it's time to depart? How do we find the path to the sea?

■ ■ ■

Answering the Call to the Sea

Today, when we think of exploring a new path, we recognize that we are more vulnerable and that life is more difficult than we had been led to expect. There is a widespread sense among many people that everything that was once tied down is coming loose.

On September 11, 2001, the world absorbed a devastating act of darkness. Suddenly, we were forced to think deeply about what matters most in our lives. When faced with a crisis this immense, matters of purpose could seem trivial. But the truth is that the question, "For the sake of what?" became the operative question of the day. Purpose was not trivial, but essential. The events of September 11 called us to the sea. They called us to ask the big question, not only so we could cope and heal, but also so we could make sense of the new world we're living in. The tragedy brought forth the question in firefighters, rescue workers, and ordinary people who dropped everything simply to serve. Their deeds were a witness to our intrinsic purpose and a clear answer to the question, "For the sake of what?"

It is a great tragedy that the big question is never asked by many except in a crisis. And when we are confronted with a crisis, then we are given a choice to answer the call, to fulfill our highest purpose. What matters are the choices we make in a crisis.

Purpose is our answer to the question, "For the sake of what?" Our answer is crucial to our health and happiness. Our bodies need messages of hope from the brain to cope and to heal. Those of powerful purpose have always known this. They have understood that a meaningful life must somehow celebrate the purpose that life provides. They have understood what the great South African playwright Athol Fugard wrote: "The only thing that ever matters in the world is what one person does or says to another person."

After twenty-seven years in prison, Nelson Mandela knew this. He demanded dignity for himself and his people and got it because he was centered in the big question. Despite his stature as one of the most admired people in the world, Mandela never lost his sense of the African tradition of *umbuntu*, described by retired Anglican archbishop Desmond Tutu as "a person is a person through other persons."

■ ■ ■

Purpose Requires a Mind and a Body

Purpose is rarely handed to us. We get it by choosing to have it. We get it by embodying it. A sense of purpose comes from within. Only we know if we have it. Only we know if there is something in our life that makes us want to take a stand.

Purpose requires a mind and a body that work together, an integrated mind/body state. I'm drawn to people who embody passion and purpose. When I saw Nelson Mandela speak many years ago, I felt affirmed and inspired, not because of his words but because he was fully present with me. The man smelled of purpose.

Heeding the call to become president of South Africa, Nelson Mandela said of himself, "I was not a Messiah, but an ordinary man who had become a leader because of extraordinary circumstances." Surely time and circumstance favored Mandela in distinct ways. He leaves a legacy like few others in world history. The power of his purpose places him beside twentieth-century giants like Mahatma Gandhi and Dr. Martin Luther King Jr. Like them, Mandela risked his life for the sake of dignity as he sought to overthrow a white police state with a well-equipped army. Unlike Gandhi and King, however, he lived to see his legacy. No one will be able to deny Mandela his legacy: "I want to sleep for eternity with a broad smile on my face. I want those who remain behind to say this man has done his duty."

It takes centering to live on purpose. The authority of Nelson Mandela reflected a deep knowing of center. Being centered allowed him to tell the truth in a simple way. From a centered way there was no need for him to exaggerate his own importance in order to win approval. He knew very clearly that who he was was enough.

How will we know we're enough? The world is a great and mysterious place, and it contains more paths to the sea than our minds can conceive. The single most important step we can take is to live authentically enough to be tested and challenged by the question of destiny, the question "For the sake of what?"

Centering is a simple art available to us all. We each have the capacity to organize body, mind, and spirit in a way that makes us more present, more hopeful than ever before.

■ ■ ■

Marathon of Hope

Terry Fox is a clear example. The need to answer the big question was thrust upon this young Canadian early in life. Two days after his eighteenth birthday, Terry learned he had a cancerous tumor in his right knee. His leg would have to be amputated immediately or the cancer could spread through the rest of his body. Suddenly life was tentative, no longer to be taken for granted. Despite the shock and the speed with which Terry's life had changed, he spent little time in the trap of self-pity. Within the confines of his hospital room Terry detected his purpose, his personal answer to the "for the sake of what?" question.

Most of us will be forced to answer the question when we experience life crises. But as Terry Fox put it, "You don't have to do like I did—wait until you lose a leg or get some awful disease—before you can take the time to find out what kind of stuff you're made of. Start now. Anybody can."

Two weeks after his surgery, Terry began chemotherapy. The cancer clinic and the painful treatments were a reminder to Terry that almost half of all cancer patients never recover. Terry could no longer take his life for granted. He decided he wanted to do something for the people who were still at the clinic. He began to determine what it was he cared deeply about, what moved him. Terry began to discover a new sense of purpose. He would run all the way across Canada to raise one million dollars to fight cancer. He would give the money to the Canadian Cancer Society.

Months later, Terry dipped his artificial leg in the ocean off Newfoundland and began his epic run. After running three-fifths of the way across Canada—a marathon a day for five months—Terry Fox had to leave his Marathon of Hope. The power of purpose had transformed an average athlete into a person who, with an artificial leg, ran a marathon a day. He never finished. The cancer had spread to his lungs. By the time of his death, one year later, he had raised many millions of dollars and had inspired hundreds of thousands of people.

Terry Fox had a profound impact on my life. While camping around the perimeter of Lake Superior, I came upon him running just outside Thunder Bay, Ontario. Sandwiched between the flashing red lights of a highway patrol car and a van with a "Marathon of Hope" banner on its side was Terry Fox, a man with a centered purpose. There is no true hope without center. Terry embodied hope. Whenever the art of centering is practiced, things change dramatically. That unexpected meeting changed the course of my own life dramatically.

Terry Fox challenged me with that centered look. He made me ask, "For the sake of what am I living my life?" He made me realize that I needed to embody a purpose by which I could deliberately guide my life. I began to shape a new vision for my work. I would dedicate myself to helping people uncover their calling.

■ ■ ■

Claiming Your Purpose

Purpose is not something that is granted to one person and not another. Neither is it reserved for only the great or near great. It is not something impractical or mystical. When you come from center, you can be courageous. You are secure in yourself, in your deep connection to the ground you stand upon. Therefore, you can step out in life answering the questions "How can I contribute?" and "How can I make a difference?"

Perhaps we were placed on earth to meet the challenge of a single day; perhaps, like many ordinary people in New York City, to respond to a devastating disaster. Or maybe our purpose is to change the world like Nelson Mandela to raise millions to fight cancer like Terry Fox.

Like a path, purpose must be walked. Our purpose is determined by one thing and one thing only: the degree to which we add to or subtract from other people's lives. The degree to which we dare to fully live in the question, "For the sake of what?" The degree to which we are willing to say "yes" to what truly matters to us.

Centering ourselves from the essential question allows us to feel our passions and at the same time gives us the strength to take action from our highest purpose. Centering is always a choice we can make. Centering works.

When they sense a path or face a crisis, people like Nelson Mandela, Terry Fox, and countless others give themselves to it with their bodies, minds, and spirits. They embody the practices of centering that strengthen them to get up every single day saying "yes" to what matters most in their lives.

Purpose is a path to the sea that has been taken before, and the path is well trodden for those who dare to follow it. In my thirty years as an executive coach, I have observed that having a purpose is the single most significant predictor of life fulfillment. Having a purpose is one of the critical factors in emotional intelligence, considered by some to be a better predictor of success than technical knowledge or general intelligence.

Purposeful people have made three simple yet profound choices in their lives. First, they see their part in the scheme of things. They sense their special place in the grand pattern of life. They do their part by choosing to leave the well and following their own path to the sea. It's often a different path. It's the historic path Thoreau captured when he wrote, "If a man does not keep pace with his companions, perhaps he hears a different drummer." Second, they see that no problem ever comes to them that does not have a teaching in it, that cannot contribute to their spiritual growth. They choose to see problems as opportunities in disguise. They know that if they did not have friction, they would drift through life. They recognize that we need friction to grow. Third, they see that the path to the sea is a path of service. Serving others is what they choose to make their lives about. Our motive, if we are to be truly happy, must be an external motive—it must be service. It must be giving, not getting. When we live to give instead of to get, we step onto the path to the sea.

Terry Fox symbolized what most of us want to know: that there is a purpose to life, that our being here does mean something, and that what we do matters. Behind any great deed is at least one individual who was consumed by the hope that he or she could make a difference in the world. People like Terry Fox and Nelson Mandela learn to move the focus of their attention away from themselves to others. They learn to let life question them.

There is in each of us, no matter how humble, a purpose. We are all part of the human family. We all have a place in this world. There is no tragedy so great, no life so small, that we cannot answer the big question, "For the sake of what?"

No amount of walking on the path will reveal with certainty our place in the world. Purpose demands hope. It is a mystery. Anne Morrow Lindbergh captured that mystery in her book *A Gift From the Sea* when she wrote, "I would like to achieve a state of inner spiritual grace from which I could function and give as I was meant to in the eye of God." When we come to the edge of the sea, and the issues that so consumed our lives recede from us like waves from the beach, it will be our daring answer that will become our gift to the universe.

Part Two

Leading the Way

Chapter 2

The Leadership Dojo:
Leadership as a Path of Awakening
∼ Richard Strozzi-Heckler

For the past three decades I have been working with the military, Fortune 500 companies, government agencies, entrepreneurial technology companies, and utilities groups in the United States, Canada, Europe, and Latin America to develop programs in team building and leadership training called the Leadership Dojo.™ These programs have demonstrated that leadership is a skill that can be learned and institutionalized within organizations. In the Leadership Dojo we work with the premise that the "self" is the leader's primary source of power. Clearly, intellectual capacity and specific technical skills matter, but alone they do not make a powerful, effective leader. We have seen time and time again that the self that one is ultimately decides one's success as an exemplary leader. Furthermore, we submit that the body is indistinguishable from the self. This is not a trivial statement; it is essential to include the body if one wants to build the skills of exemplary leadership.

In this chapter I will write first about the learning environment of the Leadership Dojo and then about the role of the body and the "self" in leadership.

■ ■ ■

Dojo: A Place to Train

The term dojo is from the Japanese traditional arts and means the "place of training." Its origin is the Sanskrit word bodhimanda, which translates as "place of awakening." From this we can gather that since humans have recorded their history they have evoked the importance of coming together in a place in which they can wake up, learn, and transform themselves. A dojo, then, is a place to awaken to and learn new ways of being in the world. In a dojo students traditionally practice a specific art with other students under the direction of a qualified teacher. While the students learn and gain competency in a specific discourse, like martial arts, flower arranging, theater, or the tea ceremony, for example, they also build the foundation for a moral, ethical, and spiritual life. In other words, they begin to evolve as people. As they learn a particular art or skill they also, over a period of time, learn the universal principles necessary for producing personal mastery, social dignity, and pragmatic wisdom. In the case of the Leadership Dojo a specific skill—making strategic assessments, for example—is learned, while at the same time the self that one is matures and evolves. In this way character values and pragmatic skills are joined as a powerful leadership presence. This is what it means to be on a "Path of Awakening."

■ ■ ■

The Importance of Practice

A fundamental claim of the Leadership Dojo is that the cultivation of the self, which is the foundation for exemplary leadership, occurs through engaging the body in recurrent practices. This runs contrary to our common sense, which tells us that by reading a book or going to a weekend seminar we will suddenly have the capacity to perform differently. In the

Leadership Dojo the emphasis is on practices that allow us to embody new skills and to act in new ways.

As an example, consider a martial arts dojo where the focus is on learning to resolve conflict through perfecting certain techniques (a physical skill) and cultivating the presence to employ the appropriate force at the appropriate time (an ethical and decision-making skill). In the dojo environment it is understood that these competencies and virtues come to maturity through recurrent practices, not by academic learning. In other words, it isn't assumed that one will automatically absorb the sensibility and skills necessary to be a warrior by merely reading books, studying CDs, or watching classes at the dojo. What is required is that one place oneself under the direction of a competent teacher, alongside other committed students, to train toward mastery. The notion of practice—completing the moves over and over again, with awareness, so they become available (embodied) when needed—is critical. In the same way we emphasize practice in the Leadership Dojo, so that one can not only learn the specific techniques required to fulfill professional commitments such as sales, management, product development, and marketing, but also develop the more ontological leadership skills of meaning, purpose, relationship and team building, and culture.

■ ■ ■

New Interpretation of Body

When I speak about training the body I do not simply mean the physical body as a motor system, or the rationalistic notion of the body as a collection of parts—legs, lungs, muscles, nerve endings—but a domain of action, mood, learning, and coordination with others. Training the body in this sense doesn't mean losing weight, building big biceps, having a flat stomach, or developing the ability to hit a golf ball a long way; it means training the self to be an effective and ethical leader.

Body is used here in the somatic sense of the word. *Somatics,* from the Greek, refers to the living body in its wholeness. This is the human possibility of harmonizing body, mind, emotions, and spirit. What somatics proposes is a fully integrated individual who embodies athletic prowess, emotional maturity, and a spiritual sensibility. As the poet William Blake said, "There is no body distinct from the soul." This is not the sleek, airbrushed body on magazine covers or the Cartesian notion of body as beast of burden that ferries a disembodied mind to its intellectual appointments. Nor is it the mechanical, physiological body of modern medicine or the religious formula of flesh as sin. Somatics envisions responsible citizens that have the physical, emotional, and moral commitment to work and live together in integrity and dignity. These citizens are persons of feeling, authenticity, and commitment whose emotional range encompasses everything from gentleness to the rage of indignation. The body expresses our history, identity, roles, moral strength, moods, and aspirations as a unique quality of aliveness we call the self. These virtues mature when they extend beyond the individual self and create communities of ethical cooperation. This is the wisdom of 500,000 years of biological evolution. The body we are *is* the life we live.

■ ■ ■

Embodied Knowledge vs. Intellectual Knowledge

Because dojo learning is characterized by placing our bodies, over and over again, in practices, it runs counter to our conventional educational system. In the dojo the teacher declares the subject being taught and then speaks to what concerns it addresses in the students' world. Then through a demonstration the teacher reveals the subject in action for the students, and then the students practice. The focus is on the practices and the coaching of the teacher. This is radically different from sitting passively and listening to a lecture or studying charts and diagrams. Learning is possible in a lecture hall, but it leads to academic knowledge rather than embodied knowledge. Academic knowledge is an intellectual understanding; it fills the head with information. According to this model we say that someone has learned something if they can understand and analyze data. This type of learning has its place, but it is not necessarily designed to enable effective leadership. Embodied knowledge, on the other hand, is the ability to act appropriately at the appropriate time. It is immediate, available, and responsive. Academic knowledge does not live in the present moment; it is stored in theories, books, and computer chips. Embodied knowledge occurs through recurrent practices, not with memorization or rote learning. This is not an argument against theoretical learning; it is a declaration that learning in the Leadership Dojo leads to the capacity to take new actions. We are now at a historical crossroads, and it is crucial that learning be placed in a context of action, as a way of being in the world.

▦ ▦ ▦

Building a Leadership Presence

Consider the experience of Paul, a newly appointed sales manager for a large technology company. Paul had been highly successful in sales, but he lacked a background in leading a team or delivering presentations to upper management. In his new position he was well prepared in his research, but when he gave presentations he was thrown into a state of anxiety. He constantly fidgeted, tugged at his tie, stuttered, and broke out into a sweat. His discomfort drew more attention than his report. People had a hard time following him, and they began to distance themselves from him. His anxiety spread to others, and it had an overall negative effect on his team. He was unable to motivate or mobilize others; he couldn't bring his teammates into alignment. He appeared afraid, out of contact with others. He was smart and well meaning, and he sincerely cared for people, but his body betrayed him and he was caught in a repetitive cycle of isolation and failure. Realizing this could jeopardize his career, he read books on stress, attended a workshop on public speaking, and eventually saw a counselor. This made him more aware of the causes of his anxiety, but it did nothing to shift his performance. This increased his distress and he became increasingly resigned.

When he and his team began the Leadership Dojo he was introduced to practices that allowed him to perform differently, rather than make himself "better." He learned what it meant to center himself so that his actions and behavior were consistent with what he cared about. He learned to identify the sensations, breath patterns, and muscular organization that immobilized him. Identifying these patterns allowed him to quickly *return to center*, a state where he was present to others, open to possibilities, and connected to himself and what he cared about. He did this by dropping his breath to his abdomen, relaxing his body without going slack, and moving his attention from his thoughts about performance to feeling himself. Learning how to become a *centered presence* enhanced his self-awareness and awareness of others, increased his ability to listen to others, and built his skill in generating positive moods. Others began to trust him more as they saw he was more relaxed and present. Their confidence in him was restored and the team gained alignment and momentum.

Because the point is so simple it bears repeating: Paul learned new ways of acting by putting himself into new practices that changed his behavior, not by reading books or memorizing a formula for success. These practices included centering practices with himself and his teammates: he had frank and direct conversations with his team; he began to pay attention to the breath patterns in himself and others; and he saw how moods like resignation, resentment, and possibility lived in his posture and comportment. He saw how this produced identities that either opened or closed possibilities. Over time he even developed his ability to coach his team members around individual performance and enhanced team cohesion. The practices from the Leadership Dojo became a standard routine for his team and it was remarked upon how their business processes and mood had dramatically improved. He is still nervous before presentations, but he can now work with the situation through his centering practice.

It is important to note that the practices in Leadership Dojo include the specific conversations, actions, and issues that the individuals and teams are dealing with in their organizations. One does not learn leadership in a vacuum as an intellectual exercise for its own sake. Leadership is a social phenomenon that has meaning inside of an already existing set of commitments and anticipated future concerns. While participants learn the fundamental embodied practices of an exemplary leader in the Leadership Dojo they are doing so as they take care of the business at hand. It is not in a retreat situation that one embodies the virtues of leadership, but in the heat and liveliness of the very issues that require one's leadership.

■ ■ ■

The Self in Leadership

The development of the self in the Leadership Dojo is not to be confused with self-esteem training, personality development, or self-improvement seminars. Our interest is not in getting better or fixing oneself but in performing with mastery. Self-esteem training concerns itself with producing positive self-regard. It is a process that results in one feeling better about oneself, but it does not necessarily lead to new actions or improved performance. The leadership path of self-cultivation in the Leadership Dojo is concerned with developing leaders who embody the ethics of individual responsibility, social commitment, and spiritual legacy. It is a rigorous discipline that has its roots in two ancient traditions, from the East and the West.

In the Western tradition, Aristotle, in his *Rhetoric*, speaks of *ethos*, a type of leadership that is "a form of influence that causes other people to change their values and so their performance of tasks." He goes on to explain that ethos is a leadership virtue distinct from rhetoric or persuasive language. Ethos is not what a person says or promises but a way of being in the world. It is a presence and comportment that influences others to follow and to be open to the leader's ideas. The words of William Shakespeare come to mind: "By my actions teach my mind." This implies that the fundamental and distinguishing elements of an individual's character, as observed in their countenance, have the power to mobilize and change another's outlook and performance. When someone is the embodiment of ethos those around them act with velocity and conviction. Ethos is not simply an intellectual principle of character but a living bodily presence. In this state people have the strength to take a stand for what they care about as well as the flexibility to adapt to a changing world. Ethos is the opposite of pathos, which arouses one's pity and sympathy. Ethos arouses respect, mobilization, and action.

In the Eastern tradition, *shugyo* consists of two Chinese characters, meaning "to master" and "a practice." Literally, then, it means "to master a practice." In everyday speaking, however, it is understood as self-cultivation. In this tradition the goal is to discipline one's spirit, or character, by using one's body. In a general sense the activity is not what is important: the practice could be walking, running, yoga, swimming, or even golf. It is the intention behind the practice that produces the meaning. Shugyo, or self-cultivation, carries the meaning of developing the human spirit through physical practices. This is not to be mistaken with the modern Western sports goal of developing the motor capacity of the body while ignoring the power of mind/body synchronization. Shugyo has the goal of achieving a mature personality that can generate positive emotional states and control negative ones. This is a different end than the sports objective of strengthening the body so that it can successfully perform certain movements.

The practices of shugyo are designed so the personal self will ultimately be absorbed into the world self. Although this may initially sound vague and amorphous, it simply means that it is a leadership virtue to master one's personal wishes, cravings, and desires for the sake of a larger commitment. Shugyo reflects the importance of going beyond the appetite of the self-centered ego if one wishes to gain mastery, live an exemplary life, and lead people. In this state the body is relaxed, the mind is free of self-conscious thoughts of success or failure, and one's energy or intention flows freely, without obstruction. There is a balance between pushing forward and hanging back. From this centered presence one can act directly and appropriately to take care of the situation at hand. This state of body/mind synchronization is more effective than the personal, centralized self. The result of shugyo is pragmatic wisdom, a self that is not driven by compulsion, fear, or self-interest but instead acts for the greater good.

The following case study exemplifies how cultivating the self produces a leadership sensibility that contributes to the success of the entire enterprise.

Jerry is the CEO of a successful international leasing corporation that he founded fifteen years ago. He received his MBA from a prestigious university, and before starting his own business he was the executive vice president of a Fortune 100 company. His traditional business credentials are impeccable. His fellow students at business school admiringly called him "Patton" for his hard-driving approach. For the first five years Jerry's company thrived and grew an average of fifteen percent a year. Then began a leveling-off period, which resulted in a stall that affected profits and morale. He tried to "fix" this downturn by increasing his autocratic command-and-control style of leading. Some of his best talent began to leave, and it became questionable whether the company would survive. In the words of one of his managers, "He responded to the increased pressure by turning up his volume and turning down his listening. He became more demanding and he was increasingly shrill and harsh. This alienated people in the company and our customers began to see him as needy and desperate. He was hard to be around."

When he came to see us he was looking for tips and techniques to fix his management and sales teams. He saw the problem as outside himself, something that technology or a systems change could solve. When we told him that it was necessary that he first examine his leadership style he was taken aback. It had never occurred to him that he might be part of the problem. "After all," he said, "look at my history of success. Why do I need to change?" Jerry lived in a world in which mood, passion, relationships, and the joy of team collaboration didn't exist. His business acumen, the marketplace, and his hard-driving style had allowed him to succeed up to this point without engaging in these fundamentally human issues. But he was now at a crossroads that required that he transform his leadership style or fail. I initially worked with Jerry individually, and then he and his management team participated in a Leadership Dojo.

Jerry and his team went through three phases in their work with us. In the first phase their historical way of being in the world, as individuals and as a team, was revealed to them. This illuminated the different patterns, both positive and negative, they automatically fell into with each other. Observing themselves from this perspective made them less reactive to each other and more accepting of their individual strengths and limitations. They could see which traits were useful and which were simply conditioned responses that no longer had value for their business mission. They learned this by interacting physically in practices appropriated from the Japanese martial art of aikido and somatics. They weren't doing martial arts but engaging in physical practices that revealed their styles to each other. This is more powerful than taking a standardized personality test like Myers-Briggs as it allows participants directly to feel and experience their patterns of behavior. One's embodied history then is not simply an intellectual idea but something that one can observe. For Jerry and his team there now existed a choice where before there had been only unexamined reaction. This created a trust out of which more effective collaboration and cooperation practices were possible.

In this stage Jerry was able to see how he created a mood of resentment and resignation within the company; he and his team also saw how their automatic reactions affected the way they related to customers and the marketplace itself. It became obvious that Jerry's personal style had become a company style and it hindered the way management moved with business opportunities. They saw how much their recent failures had to do with how they mismanaged their relationships with customers and how they had missed possibilities in the marketplace.

In the second phase we implemented relational practices and business processes that were necessary for them to succeed at the individual, team, and company level. This included structured conversations that ranged from intimate conversations about personal style and history to tactical and strategic business conversations. We engaged in movement practices that increased their capacity for coordination in business processes. They learned to be direct with each other in a way that enhanced both their dignity and their success as a business team. We taught them how to receive and deliver assessments that produced action and collaboration. It is important to note that these conversational practices were not simply following a script or learning a recipe of "ten easy steps." They practiced speaking to each other from a centered presence in which they paid attention to mood, dignity, and capacity. Their trust deepened, making it possible for them to strategize and innovate in ways they never thought possible.

In the third phase they engaged in practices of reading and anticipating the world. This allowed them to perceive each other, their customers, and their marketplace from a fresh perspective. They investigated marginal discourses that challenged their traditional belief systems; they had conversations with those who could articulate the historical forces that were shaping the world; and they engaged in movement practices to shape an identity that would produce success in a fast-moving world. Building on the foundation of trust and cooperation they had developed in the previous two phases, they were able to speculate, collaborate, and innovate in new ways. This kept their thinking vital and their movement in the marketplace agile and flexible.

During our work with Jerry he learned how to manage his moods and more effectively listen to his employees and customers. He was able to recruit and retain ambitious new people. His management team learned processes that allowed them to coordinate and collaborate more power-fully together. The company turned around and once again became a leader in their field. During this same period they also added new technology and became successful in Internet commerce, but Jerry's report, as well as that of his colleagues, was that the company's success couldn't have hap-pened without the change in him and his team.

■ ■ ■

In their final evaluations Jerry and his team noted significant improve-ment in these areas:

- An executive presence of integrity and authenticity
- The capacity to generate and manage moods to create a productive and balanced life
- The ability to cultivate, manage, and repair trust
- The ability to coordinate effectively with others.
- The ability to motivate and mobilize others
- The capacity to stay emotionally balanced in times of adversity and change
- An ability to listen more deeply to the concerns of internal and exter-nal customers
- The ability to resolve conflict more effectively

These skills of leadership may seem obvious to the point of being ele-mentary—certainly they are commonly seen as the necessary social skills for a leader—yet it is rare to be in an environment in which there exist prac-tices that develop them. The Leadership Dojo addresses how this knowl-edge is translated into performance.

Although the emphasis in the Leadership Dojo is on building the skills for exemplary leadership and team enhancement, there are also principles structured into this learning environment that form the internal culture of an organization. These principles become the ethics, or ways of doing business with internal and external customers. These principles are the integrity between speech and action (telling the truth to customers and colleagues); proper respect and obligation to the teacher (customer, boss), to fellow students (colleagues), and to the dojo (workplace) itself; synchronization of mind and body (making and fulfilling commitments); honoring tradition (business processes) while being open to innovation; taking a stand for one's position without arrogance or aggression; a lifelong commitment to learning; and maintaining a proper equilibrium between self-gain (career) and the concerns of the community (corporate vision). These principles are always present when training in the Leadership Dojo and inform the background ethics, morals, and norms of the company.

These distinctions are useful in start-ups that are building a corporate culture from the ground up, or in companies that are merging with others with different cultural backgrounds. An example of this blending of cultures is when Curt, a professor of computer science, produced a CD-ROM for the educational market. His product was an interactive CD-ROM for medical students to learn the anatomical, physiological, and skeletal systems of the body. With the help of a committed board and investors Curt started his company with eighteen employees. The product showed great possibilities but the business quickly ran into difficulties. He put together a group of people who were bright and competent in their roles but who were unable to act as an aligned team. They had come together from widely different cultures, from large multinational corporations to technological start-ups to recent MBA graduates to foreign nationals. Although everyone was ambitious and well meaning there was no cohesive foundation out of which they could interact with each other. They were a bunch of all-stars doing their own thing.

In their Leadership Dojo we emphasized building a company culture as they learned a common set of business processes. They learned how they lived in different and unshared interpretations of what it meant to work and learn together. They saw how this produced many of the problems they were having. It also became clear that it wasn't enough that they were all good at what they did, because if they didn't work in unison they were unable to get their product out on time, creating a mood of resentment and despair.

To close this gap we designed conversational practices that included embodying shared interpretations of accountability, commitment, and responsibility. They trained to be empathetic and direct with each other. They learned to declare breakdowns in a way that took care of their dignity and the dignity of others. They began practices that centered them on enhancing their individual careers as well as building a team committed to the success of the enterprise. From this foundation we began to look at the overarching vision they had for their lives and for the life of the business. These practices opened their humanity and produced a trust that increased their overall effectiveness.

Curt's company now employs more than 120 people and is positioned to become a publicly traded company. As new people come to the company they join the Leadership Dojo and are trained in the values of the organizational culture.

When we learn through our bodies in an environment like the Leadership Dojo we learn the social skills necessary for leadership, and we reap the inestimable benefits of interacting face-to-face with our colleagues in this virtual age. Over time the steps necessary to learn and transform ourselves become embodied, and we then can see how we can help others learn and change. Our ability to coordinate with others is increased and we become more capable of shaping a future that takes care of our personal and professional concerns. We increase our value to our colleagues and customers. The need to adapt and transform ourselves in today's world is cause for a revolution in how we learn.

Humans are a work in progress that began as single-cell protoplasms three billion years ago. One hundred thousand years ago we stood as Homo sapiens, and now we extend our influence far into the galaxy and deep into the soul of man. As moral agents we can guide the human trajectory to include the best of technology while cultivating the practices that sustain our biological wisdom. But if we continue on our present course we will doom our creativity and erode our instinct for self-generation. The moment has come, the choice is ours, and all around us we hear the call for a revival of our humanity. Together let us commit to the practices that produce a leader of pragmatic wisdom, skillful action, and grounded compassion.

Chapter 3

Embodied Leaders Changing Low-Income Communities

~ Judith Rosenberg

S ince 1991 I have been the executive director of TEAMS: Transformation through Education and Mutual Support, a nonprofit agency whose mission is to promote healthy, self-reliant communities in which people assist one another to achieve their individual and collective goals. I have been exploring the idea of the mind/body continuum for a number of years, and I have maintained a small somatic psychotherapy practice in addition to my other work.

■ ■ ■

The Need for a New Approach to Community Change

America's low-income communities are very troubled places. The problems are well documented: unemployment, inadequate housing, failing schools, poor physical and mental health, crime—the list often appears to be end-less. Most people agree that something needs to be done, and that what-ever has been done hasn't worked.

Over the last five decades the dominant approach to community change has been to improve services in the areas of health care, education, and employment. The primary instigators of change are government and nonprofit service providers, and the strategy of choice is to create more and better service-delivery programs. Based on my experiences, however, even if you succeed in making organizational changes, it is not likely that your success will result in any real change for individuals in low-income communities. By the time the policy directives filter down through the various layers of bureaucracy, from the decision makers to the line workers, the initial impetus for change is largely diluted. What this approach omits is the self-organizing capacity of poor people themselves.

■ ■ ■

New Approach: Self-Determination

In TEAMS's approach to community change, the primary goal is self-determination; the primary instigators of change are the residents of those communities; and the strategy of choice is to help people develop their capacity to help themselves and each other. Once this process of self-motivated, self-directed change begins, it is continuous and ongoing. I am not talking about isolated individuals, but about connected individuals and their families, their friends, the people they help and get help from—in other words, their social networks.

When self-determination is the primary goal, other goals, such as making improvements in housing, health care, education, and employment, are secondary. By "self-determination" I mean that poor people must define their own problems and opportunities, and set their own goals. They are the chief "doers" in any change process; they design and implement the process; and they are in control of the resources.

■ ■ ■

The Strategy:
Human Capacity Development

If the goal is self-determination for low-income communities, and the primary agents of change are poor people themselves, then the strategy of choice is capacity development for individuals and their social networks. Human capacity development is an evolutionary process of cooperative learning that is self-directed and based on meaningful action in the world.

For example, economic capacity development is not primarily about acquiring more money, or even about getting jobs and building financial assets. These things are specific *outcomes* of economic capacity development. The capacity development *process* is about building people's ongoing ability to acquire or create jobs and financial assets, the ability to manage them, and the ability to make effective and ethical use of the money they generate.

If a person or group solves a particular problem without developing capacity, it will be difficult to sustain the solution, and no easier to solve the next problem. On the other hand, if that group develops its general capacity, even if it fails to solve the immediate problem, it will be in a much better position to tackle the next issue that confronts it.

TEAMS focuses on four core elements in developing human capacity:

■ Peer support to build the basis for ongoing connection and teamwork

■ Goal-setting skills and mutual accountability

■ A process of learning through action and continual assessment

■ Direct access to resources not limited by categorical funding streams

■ ■ ■

The Support Action Team Model

At TEAMS, we have developed a model, the Support Action Team, incorporating these four elements. Facilitators recruited from the community each recruit a team of friends and neighbors who meet twice monthly to identify their individual and collective goals and support one another in achieving them. The teams create a safe and trusting environment in which personal supportive relationships are formed before the group focuses on accomplishing tasks. Exercising their leadership by undertaking group-initiated projects, Support Action Team members learn and develop confidence in their community-building and individual skills, such as team building, public speaking, understanding group behavior, time management, and community accountability and evaluation.

The basis for the development of capacity within the Support Action Teams is a process of continual learning, which incorporates somatic education and practices. Team members learn by doing and by analyzing together what works and what doesn't. Team members start by applying this new way of being to their personal lives, offering each other support and encouragement. By integrating somatic work into the learning process, people are able to make deep and lasting changes. After six to eight sessions each team identifies an issue in their neighborhood that is important to them and designs a focused, local response to this issue.

For example, team members in an inner-city neighborhood without access to a supermarket, and therefore adequate and affordable nutrition, may decide to form a food cooperative. Or parents of children in middle school may decide to create an after-school tutorial group for children whose parents work, to help reduce gang participation, promote the likelihood of graduation, and improve students' life prospects. Each Support Action Team has access to funds to implement its projects. Working together, members practice the skills they have learned, continually revising their plans to stay on course to achieve their goals.

Each Support Action Team project is designed from the outset to place emerging leaders in decision-making positions within the wider community, on civic and nonprofit boards, planning councils, and so on. To encourage productive discourse, TEAMS provides training and support not only to team members but also to governing and advisory boards on ways to bridge cultural and class differences. This establishes from the outset that community members serve on an equal footing with others and creates a milieu where all parties can learn from each other.

■ ■ ■

The Importance of Somatics in Developing Community Leaders

Some of the women working with me as facilitators of Support Action Teams were cleaning houses or doing childcare when we first met; one was homeless and working at a fast-food restaurant. None of them had jobs that truly used their capacities as human beings. In their time working with TEAMS all have moved forward in their work, taking on additional responsibilities and increasing their earning power. They are now employed as outreach workers for new parents, parent liaisons in their local schools, director of a neighborhood center, and community coordinators in family resource centers and for their city government.

How did these transformations take place? I believe that a mutual commitment to work together to achieve their goals is the central factor in this change, but that without the support of self-development through the somatic practices that I will describe the process would be much slower and much more difficult.

■ ■ ■

Core Skills for Somatic Learning

The first, foundational skill is paying attention, or learning to recognize your own somatic state. The facilitators learn that the shapes we take—our expressions, postures, and habitual ways of holding ourselves in our bodies—deeply affect our moods, emotions, and experiences in the world. By paying attention to our somatic state we learn that we are not victims but are instead creators of our own reality. Simple exercises—such as shifting your attention from your hearing to the sensation in your hands, and back again—help to develop this ability. Another exercise involves making a fist and seeing how this changes your mood. Also, by assuming a posture of being big, then one of being little, we see how our self-perception and worldview change from these different stances. Here is an example of how learning to pay attention has proven valuable for one of our facilitators.

Nyesha, a twenty-six-year-old single mother who was homeless, struggled to get off welfare and establish a solid home for herself and her young son. However, in doing so she learned habitually to hold herself very tightly in a dense, contracted, almost silent state of self-protection. Although this posture served her well in difficult situations that would normally provoke anyone to anger or despair, it also prevented her from feeling close to or making real contact with those around her, and it has left her in a chronic mood of distrust. As Nyesha has learned to recognize this state in her body, she has practiced being less contracted and silent, so that when she feels distrustful she has the choice of gently lifting her shoulders, opening her chest and throat, and speaking out to change her experience. This shift has allowed her to stop resentfully suffering in a job where she was unappreciated and to find a new job where she is loved and valued, mentoring troubled students in special education classes. It has also helped her to soften and really enjoy her interactions with her young son.

A second key skill is *centering*, learning to find a somatic home in yourself, a place of balance you can return to over and over again. Most Americans live very complex and demanding lives, trying to juggle conflicting demands of work and family in an uncertain world. In low-income communities these demands are greatly exaggerated by lack of access to adequate funds, which drastically limits people's choices as they struggle to respond to their needs and those of the people closest to them. Lack of money creates an atmosphere of turmoil and frequent breakdowns that daily throw low-income community residents off balance. In this context learning to center is crucial to becoming a leader. TEAMS facilitators practice centering by working with the breath, and by doing a standing practice of self-alignment vertically, horizontally, and between front and back. All TEAMS meetings open with this practice.

Lorena's story illustrates the importance of centering in becoming a strong community leader. She and her husband had just bought their own home after years of saving and planning. The house was a true fixer-upper and needed a new kitchen and bathroom; they had to do the work themselves to save money, living with relatives while they worked on the house. At the same time Lorena started a new job with additional responsibilities and a supervisor who micromanaged her and treated her with disrespect. The neighborhood residents who turned to her for help in her previous job still came to her for assistance. Her son was having difficulties at school. How was she to manage all this stress? Lorena turned to her TEAMS group for support and practiced centering "many times a day ... when I'd feel like I couldn't go on I'd stop and breathe into my belly and feel my weight in my feet. I'd just take a little rest and remember what's important to me. Now it's almost automatic." The house is finished, her son is back on track in school, and she's dealing well with her supervisor, in a focused, less reactive way. Lorena's family and colleagues all notice the change in her and note that she has become calmer and easier to be with.

Having learned to recognize your own somatic state and how to come back into balance, the next core somatic skill is *extending*, collecting your personal power and sending it out into the world. For most women, especially low-income and immigrant women, simply experiencing yourself as having personal power is a major shift. In TEAMS facilitators' groups we practice many different ways of creating a feeling of energy in the body and sending it to one another. We start with a distinction that every mother recognizes, that between speaking to her children in a strong, effective way versus giving them direction without any power behind it. We then expand that distinction into their work in the community. For many community leaders this is the beginning of their ability to speak out and share what they know. Without developing this capacity, attempts to involve residents in planning and evaluating community programs are bound to fail, as residents will either remain silent or say what they believe is expected of them.

Juana is an immigrant from Guatemala who has survived and thrived in her new home through great determination and commitment to her family, often working three or four jobs to save to get ahead. She is an extremely clear thinking, "no bull" kind of person, but she has learned to keep her thoughts to herself. When she first began attending community meetings with TEAMS she would rarely speak at all. Juana has worked a great deal on extending herself and speaking up. Recently, in evaluating a community event at which the professionals took over the leadership from community members, Juana was able to publicly illustrate the negative effects of the professionals' "helping." While she talked, she reinterpreted her sensations of embarrassment and blushing as a rush of energy to help her speak out. She clearly described how being bossed around made her, and everyone else, pull back and stop contributing, so that the event failed to help build the community. Juana was able to say, "they had me delivering water when anyone who needed it could have picked it up. Meanwhile, there was no one to translate when I could have helped. And there was no one to reach out to bring new members into our work." At the next community event Juana and other community members took the lead, with the professionals providing backup as requested.

Once community leaders begin to learn how to extend themselves, the next set of essential somatic skills involves learning how to work with others: creating flexible boundaries, setting limits, and *blending*. Facilitators learn that each of us has habitual patterns for how we coordinate with others (or don't). Some people usually collapse or disappear in the face of others' strength, while others will try to dominate in most situations. The facilitators learn to recognize their predominant pattern in order to develop the ability to move more flexibly in the world. In working with diverse groups, cultural differences are especially apparent in this area. What is culturally "normal" to one person may be experienced by another as intrusive or controlling, or may be seen in another culture as passive and weak. In our facilitators' groups we practice a series of exercises moving with one another, trying on roles that are unfamiliar, and acting out the part of individuals who we find particularly difficult to work with or understand.

One of the primary aspects of TEAMS's work in building community leadership is teaching residents how to set goals and be accountable to one another to achieve them. This involves learning to be open about one's limitations, learning from our mistakes, and continually moving forward together. The somatic practices involved in *making a commitment* are key in this process. The commitments to our goals, to our own growth, and to building our communities are the heart of our work together. When these commitments are experienced as something inside you rather than as someone else's expectations that must be lived up to, they have much more strength and determination behind them. For women who have been groomed as caretakers, who have been taught to focus on others' needs, it may take quite some time to discover their own internal goals and commitments. At every facilitators' meeting we report back on our goals and revise them in light of what we have learned. Each week we repeat aloud our commitments to one another, standing, centering, and speaking from the inside out.

Learning how to say no is just as important to effective leadership as making strong commitments. Facilitators learn that if we can't say no to extraneous demands we cannot fulfill the commitments we make. The somatic practice of *declining* is crucial here. Many of the natural leaders

TEAMS identifies as community facilitators have spent their lives saying yes to everyone, helping so many members of their communities that they are widely respected and appreciated. It is very difficult for them to move from being "the helper" to being a leader with clear commitments and a long-term agenda for their neighborhoods. For many, saying no brings up fears of rejection, losing opportunities, or losing positions of respect. It is often a shock to discover that we are not irreplaceable; sustainable leadership requires learning how to develop the leadership of others rather than being chronically overextended with everyone depending on us. The practices of declining are straightforward. Someone asks you for help and you say no. Facilitators learn to pay attention to the feelings that arise in saying no, and to the somatic state they adopt in order to avoid those feelings. For example, one person may make herself stiff and distant when declining someone's request in order to avoid taking in their disappointment. Another may say yes when she means no, and later let someone down when she doesn't follow through on her promises. Or, many of our facilitators keep saying yes and become frantic trying to do too much, without the time to think straight and keep on course. Learning to say no can be a truly liberating experience and the beginning of developing real leadership capacity.

Nora is an immigrant from Peru who, because of her husband's work, has had the opportunity to travel and develop a wide worldview. She is a very competent, hardworking woman who works tirelessly as a parent liaison for Spanish-speaking parents at a local middle school. She also serves on many committees and boards, and is actively involved in her own children's schools. When she first joined our project Nora would arrive at meetings gray and exhausted; she would recount her many accomplishments, but without joy. She would often seem to feel underappreciated, or even resentful. By practicing declining, Nora has discovered she can distinguish between those tasks that really matter to her and those that are beyond the requirements of her job, which she is gladly letting go of. She is spending more time with her family and is beginning to develop long-term interests and goals that satisfy her deeply. Her mood has shifted to one of happy, energetic accomplishment. Instead of overdoing she is mentoring members of her Support Action Team as they develop into leaders capable of acting effectively without her direct involvement.

The path to leadership for residents of low-income communities is not strikingly different from anyone's path of personal growth. Somatic practices are extremely valuable in the process of capacity building for community change. Being a member of a group of learners is essential in TEAMS's work. Somatic learning is ideally suited to this endeavor of mutual growth and community building because each member of our Support Action Teams is learning to live in his or her own body, and that basic human experience cuts across all lines of ethnicity, age, gender, and social class.

Chapter 4

Leading by Listening

∼ Ariana Strozzi

F illy #17 was bought at an auction. No one knew her name or her history. The only thing known about her was her pedigree, which revealed that she came from a long line of very athletic superstars in the western cow horse sports. It was possible to know more about her grandparents than about her. She displayed the same talent of movement that her line was known for. She was on the fast track to becoming a horse that nobody wanted, but she was too valuable to give up on. Besides, she was only two years old. She was sent to me because everyone else had given up on her. I was her last hope. I had a reputation for fixing problem horses and repairing a horse's willingness to partner. I've been told that the horses I've handled are known for being confident, quiet mounts, not the squiggly, goofy horses you find in many stables these days. As a horse whisperer, I work with the whole horse; the mind, body, and spirit of the horse. Having trained horses for more than thirty-five years in dressage, jumping, reining, and working cow horse, I have developed a variety of skills and techniques. Each horse is different, just as people are, and each horse reveals to me a unique personality, a set of conditioned habits, and a varying approach to making contact.

Unlike my human clients, Filly #17 could not tell me her story through words; she could only reveal herself through her actions. The only thing I could rely on was my ability to listen for her history, her story about the human, and her own sense of self. I had to listen not to what I saw on paper or heard in conversation, but to what my sixth sense said about her. I knew it was important not to let my own ideals influence the listening required to find her true nature.

I noticed her kind eye first. She was affectionate; the desire to partner was still there, but I could tell that she was lost. Her coat was soft as silk; obviously she had been well fed. Her beauty in movement inspired me. Her ears at full attention told me that she was curious and wanted to make contact. But the minute I attempted to lead her into partnership, her ears went back and she dug her hooves into the ground. Little did I know that she would be my most challenging student and teacher yet.

The weeks that followed were not easy. I applied various techniques of colt starting. I insisted she listen to me, while she just as furiously insisted I listen to her. First I focused on the simple principles of giving her clear requests, clear guidelines, and clear consequences for not teaming up with me. This failed miserably. Her bad attitude dominated every interaction. The traditional methods of colt starting were not working with her. Rather than get angry with her and force her into a mold, I remembered that she was a unique being with her own mind and her own approach to harmony. All I had to do was find it. I was determined not to lose this filly and her brilliant potential.

I knew from my years of working with horses that when I get frustrated with the horse it usually means that I have lost the game; I am being ineffective in my leadership. My goal is to create an environment for the horse in which she feels like she is accomplishing something so that I can build on that positive reinforcement. If the horse is failing, then I am failing as the leader of the team. And she was failing. So, I threw out my textbook notions about horse training and got curious. Knowing that I didn't know the answer forced me to become playful and experiment. The moment she became resistant, I knew I was missing something, and in that moment I could create a new outcome. I had great faith that by being present, open, and connected to her I could find a way to lead her to partnership. I knew my only hope for success lay in not getting caught up in the way things "should be" going. The solution lay not in fighting with her, but respecting her quirks and her fierce need for her own authority. She, like people whose trust has been betrayed in their early years, look at the world ready for the fight. The fight for self-respect and to determine one's boundaries becomes vigilance against other people's attempts to define their world. She had no respect for her human counterpart and was more focused on holding her own position than listening to my offer of a new kind of relationship.

She revealed to me that somewhere along the line her previous human had failed to lead her, had indeed confused her, and she had grown resentful of any attempt by another human to take the lead. Just like a person who is conditioned by their experiences, she held a troubled history in her sinews that presented as a mood of resentment. She had already decided that people were unreliable, dishonest, and perhaps even dangerous. Her strategy was to rebel against any attempts to stereotype her.

As I asked her to try new things, she first said, *"No, I won't, and you can't make me."* I gently encouraged her, *"I have all the confidence in the world that you can."* I worked with her body, not her mind. I had to embody confidence and consistency, so that she could learn to rely on my commitment to bring out her beauty. To do this I had to trust myself and have complete faith that she would listen back in kind. I wasn't afraid of things being messy, or trying something new. I stayed open that success may not look like my first picture of it, but if I remained flexible, she and I could find it together.

My leadership challenge with her was to reinspire her basic desire to be part of a team, to rebuild trust that had been broken, and to encourage a positive mood toward humans. I saw that any attempts toward leading her were futile as long as she lived in a mood of resentment and distrust. I knew that somehow I had to get her interested in a new game of what partnership meant or we would both feel the sting of defeat. Fundamentally, this meant I had to earn her respect first.

She reminded me of many of the human clients I have worked with over the years. I asked myself, *"Is this her mind, body, or spirit talking to me?"* Just like people, she had been conditioned by early life experiences. By looking at her patterns of behavior, performance, and perception of possibility, I could work through her habituated way of responding to life. Her sour mood and her lack of a clear story of her purpose in life had created a self-imposed wall of isolation. I knew she wanted to be somebody, to do something valuable. I could feel in her heart she wanted to change, to end her isolation.

Ultimately, my ability to lead her to a new horizon of partnership depended on my keen ability to listen deeply. It is in this somatic plain that the keys to freedom and choice lie. Whether I am working with horses or with people the somatic assets of listening, feeling, and intuitive reflection comprise a centered presence that nourish dignity and respect. I could not make her *do* anything; I could only *guide* my new friend out of the wilderness of her future.

As the weeks unfolded I slowly gained her trust. I did this through being consistent with her at all times. My mood toward her remained open and curious. When I found myself getting frustrated I would change the game. I let my intuitive mind take over and inform me of the next playing field. I stayed focused on the first and most important goal, which was getting her to become curious about me and who I was to her. I noticed that she liked to follow energy. I set up scenarios where I would ask her to listen to me; where was I going, what energy was I being? I kept grabbing her attention. As she responded with curiosity she would get rewarded and moments of bonding would happen. Our experiences of positive socializing began to build on each other and we were becoming friends.

One day I slipped onto her bareback. No saddle, no bridle. It just felt like the right thing to do. She didn't even notice. The minute my mind attempted to analyze the situation, I could feel the filly's muscles tighten and bunch, ready to spring. Each time I let go of my "knowing" mind and stayed with my animal body, without an agenda, she would soften and her ears would go forward. She started to impress me with her intelligence. I wondered who was teaching whom. She became more present than I could have hoped for. I had found the keys to her freedom.

She reminded me of a young man I worked with many years ago. Sam was a bright, handsome man in his mid-thirties. He came from a prestigious family in South America. He projected an air of entitlement that suggested people should take him seriously merely because of the family he came from. He postured that people should accept him as a leader just because he thought he had something to offer. He wanted to be granted the authority to lead (because he was born from a line of leaders), yet he had never proven his ability to do so. He resented employer after employer because they could not see his importance. He wasn't open to seeing his own reflection, to recognizing that his mood of resentment pushed away his boss and made him difficult to work with.

On a particularly hot summer day I sent Sam out to work with Sadie, a tall bay mare. His leadership task was to lead her effectively through a series of maneuvers on the ground. He had learned by doing this practice and watching others that the horse only listened to who he was being inside, not what he felt like he deserved. To my wonder this usually kind, gentle mare dropped her head, dulled her eyes, and dragged her feet around the circle. I noticed that she was going along begrudgingly in a sour mood, as if saying, "If only he were a better boss, I could be a better horse." I gently mentioned that she was being Sam and that Sam was his boss. I asked him to notice how it felt to lead a sour, resentful horse. He could see that she was not thrilled to be led by him. He could not deny the thousand pounds of mood before his eyes. Even though she was going through the moves, would he want to keep having her on his team? Did he want to promote her and give her more responsibility? I silently thanked Sadie for showing him something that other humans couldn't seem to get across.

After years of blaming others, he finally began to see how he played a part in his failing career. Sam saw through the eyes of Sadie that he presented to his employers a begrudging attitude, a notion that it was entirely their responsibility to please him. He had forgotten that to be part of an effective team he had to come to the table with a willing attitude and something to offer. He wasn't getting promoted because of the way he presented himself, not because his bosses couldn't see his value. Once we had identified the source of his breakdown in a way that he could accept, we began to work on developing a new presentation. I had him practice inspiring Sadie, encouraging her, and bringing out the 150 percent she was capable of. This new way of bringing forward his spirit of engagement would pave the way to being a team player that others would want to work with. He practiced bringing a mood of curiosity and willingness to his work and making offers that would add to the team purpose. He practiced asking his boss how he was doing and being more interested in her assessments than in his own. This was a significant paradigm shift for this young man and eventually led to him receiving the promotion that he finally earned.

The give and take of leadership resides in our flesh, in our ability to sense our environment and respond with choice. Leadership is acknowledged from the nonverbal landscape of mood, energy, and authenticity. Just like horses, people want to know that a leader will be reliable, clear in vision, part of the team, accountable, and honest. The role of leader flows from the leader to the team players and back to the leader. Leadership is a fluid, changing process. A leader who pushes his agenda on the team lacks a feeling of camaraderie, and yet a team member who digs his heels into the ground also impedes the flow of leadership. Leadership bounces back and forth between the leader and the follower. It's intangible; it isn't confined to rules or "the right way to do things." The lack of flow or harmony in a team can only be discovered by listening, not to what is said on the outside, but to what is believed on the inside.

To access this internal wisdom requires self-knowledge, self-acceptance, and clarity of one's goals and intentions. Having this emotional intelligence is only part of the whole picture. Being able to act with choice rather than "reacting" requires a commitment to practicing leadership as a physical phenomenon rather than an intellectual exercise. Developing this somatic awareness means aligning ourselves along the dimensions of mind, body, and spirit. Our mind makes sense of our environment. Our body responds to the environment. Our spirit is our underlying inspiration for possibility and meaning.

Working with horses like Filly #17 forces us into somatic-based practices because the only way we can develop communication and team partnership with them is through owning these three aspects of ourselves. When one aspect is out of integrity with the other dimensions, the horse gets lost and partnership is absent. When our mind, body, and spirit are in integrity, the horse becomes available and willing to partner. Furthermore, the reliance on nonverbal communication as the significant team-building tool forces us into practicing leadership principles rather than thinking about them. The horse offers direct feedback on whether our leadership cues are effective or ineffective.

The first step for Sam in developing a leadership presence was to identify his somatic patterns of thought, behavior, and possibility along the dimensions of mind, body, and spirit as shown in figure 1.

Figure 1. Identifying Patterns

Somatic Dimension	Patterns of
Mind	Thought Internal stories Making assessments and interpretations
Body	Behavior Performance Mood
Spirit	Perception of reality Perception of possibility

The next phase was for Sam to develop an understanding of what patterns were inhibiting his ability to progress. Once these limiting issues were identified, Sam made a set of commitments to develop new practices along the somatic dimensions listed above. Working with the horses provided a practice ground to integrate his desire for value, a willing and curious mood, and a relaxed and centered body. The feedback he received from Sadie was easier to let in and respond to than feedback from another human because Sam knew that she had no agenda for him. She was simply responding to the authenticity of his action. Figure 2 reflects the integration of more effective thought patterns and behaviors and a more responsible spiritual outlook as a result of somatic intervention.

Figure 2. Sam's Case Study

Somatic Dimension	Before Somatic Intervention	After Somatic Intervention
Mind	Interpretation #1: I am entitled to be a leader	Interpretation #1: I earn my place as a leader through my actions
	Interpretation #2: It is my boss's fault that I am not getting promoted	Interpretation #2: It is my responsibility to earn my boss's respect
Body	Mood: Resentful, begrudging; Shoulders stiff, eyes rigid	Mood: Curious, willing; Eyes soft, shoulders relaxed
Spirit	I desire to be a leader	I desire to develop myself, producing value for others through my leadership

After all my years of studying leadership and horsemanship, whether I am in the world of my animal friends or that of people, I keep coming back to the same place the poets speak of. The richness of life lies in the field of the unknowing, unexplainable sensibility of being present with what is available—the field of curiosity and flexibility. In my work with the filly, and in Sam's work with Sadie, our willingness to let go of what we "knew" in exchange for what we didn't know became the ground from which we could learn and develop new skills. I am thankful for the horse's natural ability to teach us how to listen with an authentic presence.

■ Part Three ■

Taking It to the Organization

Chapter 5

The Body of Management
∼ Robert Dunham

■ ■ ■

Lifeless Management, Organizational Pain

That the current conceptions of management and teamwork are inadequate is clear just by observing most organizations at work. Even companies that have a healthy bottom line often do not have healthy organizations, people, and moods. There is tremendous human energy and possibility being wasted in all but the very best organizations. Organizational life is for too many people a place of hope, then disappointment, of ambition, then resignation, of energy too often unused or misused, of voices ignored and a sense of disconnection. I say this from more than twenty years of experience in line management, consulting to dozens of companies and executive teams, and working with hundreds of managers and executives to strengthen their skills in management, leadership, and producing organizational excellence.

Management is largely thought of today as a set of tasks and techniques, with a strong dose of issues involving problematic people. MBA programs teach a host of analytical skills, with perhaps some active projects and communication training. But the available education tends to suffer from our cultural intellectual tradition that has us abstract things, then try to understand them. Get the theory, then apply it. But it's one thing to understand and be able to talk about, say, "courage," or "generosity," or "open listening," or "team building," and another to *do* it. In fact, we may think we understand "courage," but when the time comes for action we may find that we are not able to act in a way we consider courageous. We can't apply a theory for courage: we must be able to *act* courage, not *think* courage.

In all actions that we assess strongly as virtues and vices we act from more than our heads. We act from where we have to face our fear, our doubt, our tendencies, and our connection to or disconnection with others. We have to *feel* our way to courage. We have to find what *being* courageous is, as with love. We don't "do" love. We find what loving is in our experiences, what its feel is, its breath and energy. We then learn to go there, and going there is a continuous path of learning, and creating, what love is. In the same way, we must learn how to *be* leaders, managers, communicators, team members, and collaborators.

For most, management and organizational life are contained in a language of tasks, things to do, and results to achieve. Too often we have no language, awareness, or practices for care, for commitment, ambition, or even passion. Our cultural common sense places us in a space of thinking of using people and ourselves as mechanisms of production, not sources of energy, possibility, and drive. Too often leadership is seen as directive behavior that doesn't connect people to their own concerns and energy but instead emphasizes a sterile discipline of effort and obedience. We need a leadership of connection—connection to what people care about most deeply, to their generative energies, and to each other and their capacity to create together.

■ ■ ■

Toward Generative Leadership and Management

My colleagues and I have developed what we believe is a generative foundation for leadership and management. Its results demonstrate a powerful and effective framework for answering the question "What do I do now?" This foundation is built on awareness and attention to language and commitment, and to how they are embodied in the body. It is based on making distinctions where we have been blind, and it enables us to generate new actions that are recognized as leadership, management, teamwork, and satisfying work life. We cannot manage without the language of management and the body of management. Language that produces action, coordination, and shared commitment, which cannot happen without the body that connects to others, produces trust and can listen and be heard. These dimensions provide a generative foundation that is missing in our mainstream common sense of management and leadership. This foundation gives us new answers to the questions what is leadership and management, and how do we do them—answers that we can see, do, and learn. These answers, when engaged within authentic learning for action, enable us to go beyond our current limits.

■ ■ ■

Overcoming Our Limits

In one of our projects we worked with one of the largest software companies in the world. They had decided to form an engineering group that would provide the software components shared by all their major products. This would reduce duplication of efforts, make shared services among their products easier to design and implement, increase the quality of the products, and reduce costs dramatically. The team, about seventy engineers, was having severe difficulties. People were working eighty-hour weeks, yet they were delivering code months late, which caused tremendous lost revenue. Their code was delivered with numerous quality problems, personnel turnover was rising in the group, and the organizations they were delivering to were upset and angry due to the poor performance and lack of communication.

The problem was that the group managers were committing to more than the group could deliver because they had the impression that they "couldn't say no." First we had to enable the group managers to confront this impression and the fear and resignation that it produced. In conversations we developed a different interpretation: that committing to more than you can be sure of doing is not taking care of those you commit to. This will lead to sure dissatisfaction and trouble. Instead, we opened conversations to produce trust, to demonstrate commitment to the needs of the requesters, and to educate the requesters about the limits of capacity and of feasibility. Then, in a mood of cooperative codesign, we figured out how to best produce customer satisfaction within the limits of capacity, feasibility, and energy.

To interact with requests and demands in this way requires more than a change of ideas; it requires a change in the body, a body that can be settled, clear, and connected with demand and not driven into fear and inarticulate collapse or acquiescence. It is a reappropriation of our ability to choose when our smell of danger would have us react. We put the management team into exercises to explore how to avoid overcommitment while producing trust with their counterparts. We followed up with coaching in the team's working meetings, and in the group's meetings and conversations with their internal customers. The group managers learned how to have a new kind of conversation, make a new kind of agreement, and shift their automatic reactions in a new direction. This was not an application of ideas; it was practicing a new set of actions, skills, and emotional reflexes and blending them with other people.

As a result of learning to decline, counteroffer, negotiate, and codesign, as well as stay in regular conversations of taking care of their internal customers, the group produced a radical shift in their management practices and the results they produced. Three months later, the group produced its next delivery on time. The acceptance test found no software errors instead of hundreds of them. The group members were working with livable workloads, they hadn't needed to borrow from the work being done on the next release to make this one, and the internal customers were satisfied and complimenting the group's management team. This came from a new interpretation, new conversations, new practices, and new embodied skills in dealing with their own automatic moods, emotional tendencies, and inclinations. They had become more effective leaders and more valuable as a team, and they had produced a work life of achievement and fulfillment rather than anxiety, exhaustion, and failure.

To do this, they had to learn new skills in communication, new ways of speaking and listening. But they had to get past the words to a new embodiment of commitment and action.

■ ■ ■

The Language of Action and Creation

Leadership and management are ways of moving with others to create shared futures. To develop our abilities in doing so requires that we become aware of what we are doing, imagine how to do it better, and enter practices that enable us to actually do what we imagine. We must alter our bodies, our embodied ways of listening, interpreting, acting, and interacting.

Walter, for example, was considered a top-notch technical performer when he began to study management with us. As is often the case, his excellence in his field was considered to qualify him as a candidate for management, even though the skills of management and the skills of his technical work were largely unrelated. When he arrived he seemed quite stiff and socially withdrawn. The projects he was being asked to manage were having trouble, the people working with him had negative assessments of his work with them, and the customers his teams worked for were not satisfied. Walter was a nice guy, but he was terse, literal, and technical.

Walter had a presence of remoteness, affability, and dry logic. He tended to use his own logic when speaking to people and would lose them. He would argue for his points, but he wouldn't connect with the concerns of those he was talking to. He asked his team members to do things, but he didn't get commitments. His body was stiff and his speech chopped. The contracted way he moved in his body led me to doubt the impact we could have with him in his learning. I thought he would be a "project" and take up to two years to loosen up and embody effective management skills.

We worked with Walter in group exercises and followed up with regular coaching calls. We showed him how to explore communication, how to open to the dimensions that his technical perspective was hiding from him. As we pointed out each new dimension to investigate, it became time to learn anew.

He practiced different kinds of listening and speaking, commitments becoming central in his action conversations, and he interacted with openness to what his team members were saying and not saying. He softened, learning to extend and connect. He negotiated with people to design next steps. His team's performance improved, his customers started reporting satisfaction, and his team members began to speak positively of him. The shift was fully under way in about six months, faster than I had hoped for. But the shift came not from Walter learning in his prior analytical way, receiving ideas and then applying them. The shift came from Walter letting his body learn, from shifting his embodiment. Walter did not stay the same, and then apply new ideas. His practice shifted how he perceived, how he listened, how he spoke, and the energy of his presence. Walter shifted his embodiment, and with it his identity, results, possibilities, and his future.

■ ■ ■

The Knowledge of the Body

For thousands of years our culture has had a schizophrenic stance with respect to knowledge that hides true learning. We have two flavors of knowledge: the knowledge of what we know—understanding—and the knowledge of know-how—the ability to act.

What is the role of the body in skillful action? First, you don't have action without the body. This is a fact that we are blind to in our cultural common sense. Management, for example, is taught as abstract principles, like physics, or as anecdotes, as though description is enough to produce learning. But we cannot embody abstract ideas; we must learn the experience of the idea and translate concepts into the living shapes of our bodies in action. We must be able to articulate the actions, show the actions, practice the actions, and observe and assess the actions if we are to learn action, not abstracted ideas.

Janet, a director of marketing for a major product at a large corporation, is an example of how one can learn new distinctions and practice new actions that overcome obstacles and self-limitations. She was very frustrated with her manager, who didn't communicate on a regular schedule, gave no direction, and was rarely available. When he did get involved he seemed to mess everything up. He didn't coordinate the various departments who reported to him that had major deliverables due to her. She grew increasingly dissatisfied and frustrated, finding herself blocked by her manager's actions and inaction at every turn. Her commitments were not getting fulfilled in this situation, and, in her mind, her revenue-based bonuses and job satisfaction were going down every day. She got to the point she was going to resign and find another job. She was filled with resentment and frustration.

Janet was coached to use the situation to practice new moves. She could always leave and find a new job, but we invited her to see the opportunity for learning in the situation. She reluctantly agreed, and she found her embodied frustration was preventing her from seeing any other option than being a victim of her boss's actions. We had her examine her tendency to fall into resentful interpretations, to withdraw, and to avoid having honest conversations about the issues with her superiors. She found it difficult to calmly put her attention on her breath—an exercise for directing attention—for even five minutes. After we talked through the conversations that needed to happen, and worked with managing her tension, attention, and sensations of fear, she was able to open the missing conversations with both her manager and her manager's boss. We worked with her so that she was able to make clear requests and complaints to her manager, which at first she couldn't get herself to do. She learned to center herself and choose to take these actions rather than get lost in her resentment, anger, and fear. She found she could have conversations with her manager she didn't think she could have.

After finding that her manager would make agreements but would not keep them, she overcame another temptation to give up and took a stand with her manager's boss to get what she needed to do her job. Her reporting was shifted to another manager, and she was given permission to coordinate directly with the organizations she relied on. She began a new practice of team meetings with these other organizations, focused on clarifying and managing their promises as a team. She became an effective team leader through practicing listening, connection, and the conversations of managing commitments and breakdowns. The project went from apparent peril to a successful on-time product launch. The product exceeded revenue projections and received several industry awards, and Janet was given two other products to manage. She was able to do this without falling into overwhelm by building strong team practices and commitments. Through this process she went from working long hours to working more reasonable ones, and she made the time to get married and have her first child while continuing to manage her team.

■ ■ ■

Learning's Shift of Ourselves

True learning is a transformation of our body, of our language, of our self. It happens not only in the domain of ideas, but also in the domain of embodiment, where what we see and what we can do shifts and where our habits are changed. Our transformation shifts how we show up, how we see our future, and how we are seen by others. This definition of learning is radically different from the interpretation of learning as the acquisition of information, but it is a more accurate description of what is happening to us all the time. Learning always involves a change in our bodies, our nervous systems, and our embodiment. Our nervous system's structure is what enables us to see what we see, interpret what we interpret, and take the actions we can take. When we learn, we alter the structure of our nervous system; we see and interpret differently, and we can take actions we couldn't take before.

How do we learn? *We learn what we practice.* We *are* what we have practiced, and we *become* what we are practicing. Our practices shape our bodies and our minds, and they have been for our entire lifetime. We learn as we practice and shift our awareness, attention, interpretations, skills, and embodied capacity for action. It is important to become aware that we can choose our practices, because as managers and leaders we can practice connection and interaction that produces commitment, energy, and passion for a shared future. If we practice our old habits, we risk turning people and ourselves into raw material and mechanisms for projects, turn communication into the transfer of information, and separate our work from our care and even from people so that our work becomes a place of sacrifice instead of fulfillment. For more than twenty years I have worked with a discipline of clarifying and engaging in the elements of language that produce action and satisfaction. In all the workshops in which I have introduced these linguistic moves, people invariably find them captivating, provocative, and intensely stimulating. People experience a paradigm shift, seeing where they were blind before, and they are excited about new possibilities for their own action.

What I have found, however, is that the people in the companies where we worked would have returned to their prior habits after a couple of weeks, and the new learning and its value would have faded or disappeared. This is the result of intellectual learning, learning without the recurrent practice necessary to shifts habits, skill, and behavior. Most of our learning and education tends to be this way. The goal is to feed people new ideas, and perhaps produce positive ratings for "edutainment," but we don't produce competence in new actions and practices. The body will do what it knows, and without practice it goes back to the habits that have served it for a lifetime. But this raises the questions *What do I practice?* and *How do I practice?*

■ ■ ■

The Future Is Yours

We are the leaders and managers of our futures more than we know, whether we work in business or not and whether we have the title of "manager" or not. The skills of leadership and management are rooted in human capacities for action that we all share. Through practice we can access the possibilities of our bodies and being and become more fully ourselves in our experience of life and acting on behalf of what we care about. Through learning we can expand our ability to shape our world through practices that connect us to each other, to the wisdom of our bodies, and to our capacities to create the future.

Chapter 6

The Fundamentals of Practice

∼ Woody Allen

I started playing baseball formally with Little League one spring, and I couldn't get enough of it. I was always the first guy on the field and the last guy off. It would drive me crazy when all the other kids had to go home for dinner. After even the coach left I would throw fly balls to myself, or hit balls against the backstop, or throw balls against concrete stairs to simulate ground balls, all the while pretending I was Mickey making the great play to win the World Series. I must have broken the little finger on my left hand a dozen times making diving catches on the concrete; I never remember it hurting except when I missed the ball. Our coach would pretend not to hear the doorbell when I rang it at his apartment, a little early, every morning. I got to be pretty good at chasing down long drives in the outfield, or standing in the batters box when the pitcher was throwing a hard ball fast and close. I didn't get this way deliberately. I just loved to play, and I just loved to practice.

My nearly full-time devotion to baseball did not survive adolescence. Of course, when I was a teenager I was impervious to my coaches' assessments of my skill level; they were always wrong or biased or just stupid. I can see now that my reflexes and my batting skill weren't good enough for the first string. At the time I believed I was just as good or better than everybody else, and that the high school coaches were playing favorites, not acting on impartial assessments. And the more I believed this, the less

I wanted to play. It was a negative feedback loop of the worst kind, as the less I wanted to play, the less I cared about practicing, and the less I practiced, the worse my game got. I eventually learned some lessons from this.

I have held just about every job you can have in a business, from cleaning out pet cages at a department store to being chairman of the board of a publicly traded company. I've been a chief financial officer and a shoe salesman, an auditor and a sportscaster; I've written sales training manuals, put pins in newly made dress shirts, delivered office supplies, driven a forklift, raised private and public equity, answered the phones, mentored executives, hung toys from the ceiling of Toys "R" Us, built delivery cartons, and cleaned the central computer complex of Marriott International (for free food!). I've had experience not only with a variety of jobs, but more importantly with the people who work at those jobs.

In baseball, as in every job or sport, there are certain fundamental skills you need to have to be successful. Contrary to popular belief, very few of us are born with these skills; genetics *will* determine how tall we are, our sex, our body type, and the color of our eyes. Genetics *will not* determine whether we can hit a hot fastball or successfully lead a board of directors. These are skills that can be learned. When I started playing baseball my coach would, as part of our regular practice, have us would-be outfielders stand in the outfield and catch fly balls for as long as we could stand it. There were other drills, like throwing the ball to the right base, learning where the cutoff man was on certain balls hit to the outfield, and even practicing how many times to call for a ball that was hit in our direction. I remember my coach yelling at me, "Four times! Four times! That's how many times I want you to call for the ball!" We thought he was nuts, but many times since those early days I avoided serious injury in the outfield by adhering to that simple dictum. Call for the ball four times and the other guys in the outfield have a better chance of hearing you and can back off, lessening the chance of a full speed collision.

I learned that you couldn't just show up and be good at something. I learned it the easy way through baseball and the hard way in too many jobs. In every case, there are fundamental skills that are required, and in every case these skills are acquired through practice, with good coaching, and over time. And in every case what and how I practiced, for better or worse, became the way I *was* in that job or sport. I never got to be really good at putting pins in dress shirts (thank God!), primarily because I wouldn't listen to the assessments of the old pro on the production line. I must have stuck myself with those two-inch pins a thousand times in a month, trying to figure out on my own how to do it. I eventually learned how to stick a pin in a shirt and not my finger and produced the highest number of defects per shirt of anyone on the line. I became what I practiced: someone who could very effectively do it wrong. I have many more examples of this same "lone ranger" behavior.

I began to observe the phenomenology of *practice* as a universal experience. People were always practicing something at work or in their daily lives, whether it was how to say "hello" to the boss in the morning or how to use the new telephone in their office. The difference between baseball practice and "work" practice was that in baseball it was formally recognized as practice, and what we did at work wasn't. I began to observe that, for the most part, the notion of practice was alien in the workplace. We were supposed to show up at game time and be ready to play for our eight or nine hours every weekday having already learned, either in school or through experience, all the skills necessary to succeed. Consider that in baseball the average game time is about three hours, while the average practice time for a professional might be three times that for each game. I started thinking about other sports, such as golf and football, and I began to see the same pattern. Most athletes spend *three times* as much time practicing as actually playing the game I also noticed that what the pros practiced wasn't necessarily trick plays or special moves or shots. They spend the majority of their practice time on fundamentals like grooving their batting stroke, positioning their bodies correctly so they can catch ground balls in the optimum position, finding a smooth putting stroke, or blocking and tackling—all stuff they learned when they first started playing the game.

This is the protocol I had when I played as a Little Leaguer: fundamental drills and fundamental skills, over and over, so that when the game's on, the fundamentals are *in your body*. You don't have to stop and think "should I bend my elbow on the backswing" as you address the ball. The fundamental moves of the sport have become "embodied," or second nature. And it appears that to remain second nature these fundamental moves must be practiced repeatedly, or the "edge" disappears. As an example, think of the heart surgeon who learned his skill in medical school and then didn't actually operate on anybody for ten years. Chances are pretty good that you'd look around for somebody who was actually practicing this craft to cut you open.

When I wrote the sales training manual for a broadcasting company, we had perhaps 250 salespeople—some rookies, some seasoned vets—and a dozen or so sales managers, most of who were promoted by virtue of the fact that they had been the most productive in sales. They had embodied the moves of a successful salesperson, not necessarily the moves of a successful manager. My goal was to find those fundamentals for our salespeople to practice. I considered domains like public speaking, since that's basically what they do when they're out in the world, and the art of designing and making proposals. I considered industry-specific materials, and the importance of our sales guys knowing about the businesses they were making offers to. When all was said and done, after eighteen months of consultation, thought, and effort, we changed the way we, and for that matter the broadcasting industry, had traditionally thought of training. The manual we produced was announced with pomp and circumstance to the entire sales and management team, and it received great "press" both internally and externally. Unfortunately, it was pretty much a dud.

The two biggest complaints we heard about our proposal were, "It takes too much time," and "Most of our guys already *know* this stuff." I was initially stunned and disappointed and, reading the sales figures, I couldn't help but note that we were, at that time, heading for a disappointing year. I thought back to the number of times I had stabbed myself with the pins on the dress shirt line, and I wondered if this weren't just a more serious example of the unwillingness of people in business to practice anything, whether or not they've already "learned" it. The training manual, *A Promise for Excellence*, now sits gathering dust on one of my bookshelves, relegated to history as a really good try.

Paradoxically, I found that my notions of practice were reinforced by this episode. I started watching not only salespeople, but also accountants, production guys, on-air announcers, and engineers at their work, and I kept coming back to the idea that the best of them were always going through some ritual of practice even if they didn't call it that. Like the engineer in Pittsburgh who, first thing every day, would read his meters to make sure the radio station was on the air, even though he could hear it loud and clear over the speakers booming through the building. Or the accountant who would actually re-add his adding machine tape to make sure his machine hadn't made an error (you may have to think about that one for a minute). I began to see these as more than just personal idiosyncrasies. We all do similar things all the time. And what we do shapes us. The accountant taught the junior guys on his staff to do the same thing, and the engineer convinced his apprentices that the meters—not their ears—were telling the truth about what was going out over the airwaves. The sales guys had their own ways, which didn't include making the presentations we suggested or learning more than superficialities about a new business. Our suggestion of a new or formal practice was basically a challenge to *who they were*, and it required a new commitment to new practices. Again comparing this to professional sports, can you imagine the response of a coach if a player's response to blocking and tackling drills was, "I already know how to do that," or "it takes too much time."

This idea that we embody what we practice is not startling, but the notion that we're always practicing something all the time may be new. As an example, most of us drive a car regularly. My claim is that over time *the way* we drive becomes so built in that we don't stop to think about it at all. The shape of our bodies, the way we hold the wheel, the way we use the accelerator and the brake, the way we hold our heads so we can see the mirrors, the position of our hips and shoulders, and how we put our safety belts on are all in the background. So, for that matter, are the actual tools we're using; the steering wheel, the brakes, and the tires are rarely in the forefront of our thinking. We are, in essence, practicing how we drive all the time. Of course, we don't think of it that way. I claim that, for the most part, this is also true of the way we are at work.

My goal is to bring into the foreground what we're already doing anyway, and to produce some structure to it. In this way, we can begin to examine what we're doing in terms of:

- What are the fundamental skills I need for this position?

- How am I practicing them, or not?

- Who can help (coach) me?

- What is the game I'm practicing for?

- When am I "in the game"?

There may be other questions here that are relevant, but let's use these for starters. If we looked at the "circle" of action, we'd see something like Figure 3.

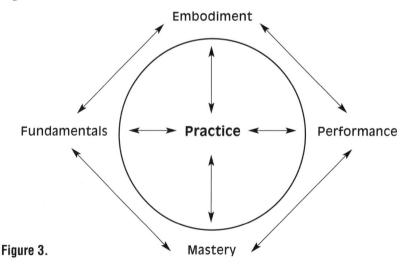

Figure 3.

If you were playing football, then some fundamental skills would be passing, catching, blocking, tackling, kicking, and running. Some practices would be running specific drills, exercise, plays, paying attention to your nutrition, learning the playbook, scouting the competition, and weight, strength, and balance training. You would engage in these practices to learn these skills and to develop competence or mastery so that your performance during the game would be sufficient to compete at a high level.

In business, some broad examples of fundamental skills might be speaking, writing, building relationships, relating to others, working with computers, and a whole host of job-specific requirements, like using a jackhammer or understanding the principles of Accounting 101. Some broad practices might be reading the trade press, regular attendance at training meetings, giving practice speeches, getting CPA certification, or responding daily to email. These skills and their related practices would produce the capacity to act effectively in the world. My goal here is not to make a list of all the fundamental skills that we need to do our jobs, or all the practices required to learn them, but, first, to pose the question of what they are and, second, to speculate as to how to formalize their implementation.

I believe the analogy between the way professional athletes go about their work and training and the way those in business go about theirs is useful and instructive, and it can produce an opening for businesses to more effectively train and grow their people and for people to more effectively prepare themselves for the game. I hold that *we are what we practice,* and that *we're practicing all the time,* even if we don't see this. I understand that practice as practice in business seems an unusual concept, since it looks like the game is being played forty to more than sixty hours a week, but we can shift this common sense. I see that there are certain fundamental skills required in any profession, and I see that the practices for honing and sharpening these in business are haphazard at best. My goal is for people to begin to notice for themselves what they're doing already and how this shapes them, and to look at what's really required to excel in their jobs. This will produce a big opportunity for new embodiment, mastery, and more wins on the scoreboard.

Chapter 7

Wringing out an Old Sponge:
Where Personal Dysfunction Meets
the Pretense of Corporate Caring

~ Tom Lutes

S teve sits in the back, in fact so far back he's almost out the door. His large white arms fold across a huge extended belly. Baseball cap tugged down firmly in place. He's real big and he's got a real attitude. His tightened jaw accentuates the glowering eyes staring out at me from deep inside his skull. He's mad. Damn mad. In fact, terminally mad, and today he's definitely in no mood to talk about it, especially not in our "little communication workshop" he was "forced" to come to. Steve's so disgusted and been that way for so long he can barely utter any words about it, except to spit out disdain for "them." He's worked thirty-two years in the coal-fired power plants of Detroit pumping out power so half the state of Michigan can keep running. His father, his brother, and two sons used to work here too.

He turns away from me, staring off into his anger. I imagine he's being carried back to the old days I've heard so much about, when people loved their work and were proud of the company, the family atmosphere, and their place in the community. But it's not that way now. Not at all. Now he just wants to get back at "them," do as little as possible, and get as much as he can. "Screwing them back" is his last remaining act of retaliation after thirty-two years of what the company calls service. "You bet!" he says.

"Get all I can and stick it to them. Over and over, as much as I can. They deserve it and more for all the shit I've had to take. Yeah, I get paid well. Damn sure better after putting up with their lies all these years."

Steve, at least in his own mind, has been consistent, reliable, and dependable, and he has put in a good day's work almost every day of those thirty-two years. He did it the right way, the way he'd learned from his father and the others. Each day they taught him to do an honest job, use good values, look after people, and follow the rules. He'd be taken care of if he did. He never wanted a career; that was for those "college types." All he wanted was a job. Just do a good job and go home. Doing the same thing for thirty years was just fine. He didn't need to improve every day, just do a good job and go home. He didn't need to be everyone's boss, just to be treated fairly for a good day's work. And that's how it was for quite a while. Then somehow the rules changed. Suddenly it wasn't enough just to show up on time and do what was expected; now you had to learn to "communicate," "diversify," and "do sissy stuff like this class."

It's hard to fault his simmering resentment, yet who can really deal with it? Certainly not the managers who hide behind layers of other managers working ever so closely with even more layers of lawyers. Steve is caught. Like so many others, he feels stuffed into some irrelevant inseam of our national grab for profits. Steve is a heartful man, yet he can feel no heart in the world of work these days.

A surly, tough survivor in a corporate culture built to reward those at the top first and those at the bottom last, he views the world entrenched behind an angry, aggressive exterior. He has stayed rigid in his hatred of management for so long that he is now frozen in place. Through the years this person who was once so young and strong has become almost brittle. Hiding behind the need for structure, certainty, and routine, people like Steve will never admit to their vulnerability. Instead they cling to the stability of their anger, bonding around a common disgust for "them."

I'm leading a one-day communication workshop. Steve is one of approximately six thousand people who will do the program in the coming four months. It's part of a multiphase, multiyear effort to begin to bridge immense communication gaps between the upper and lower echelons of the company. Born out of a desire by upper management to begin some kind of healing process, this phase of the program is for groups of union employees from the power plants. They are ordered to come, like it or not. As a result, easily eighty percent have an attitude when they walk in the door and make no bones about not wanting to be there. Speaking with similar degrees of intensity and bitterness, many tell the same stories of management's cutthroat deceit and interest in looking out only for themselves. Steve is just one of a huge number of people within this company, and around our nation, who feel that way.

We have a ten-person team of facilitators representing diverse races and gender. Each week we meet and discuss how we can work more effectively, have more impact, and better deal with the anger we face. About halfway through our sixteen-week run, our team begins to give voice to the following politically touchy observation. The difficulty of our day as facilitators always comes down to one major factor: How many "baseball caps" do we have? Although their shape and size vary, their attitude is always the same: glowering eyes, baseball cap pulled down tight, arms folded—always folded—across the chest, older, strong, male, white. We know the day will go relatively easily when we look out at our audience and see at least one-third people of color or women. These days our groups consist of very few, and we know we're in for a battle.

Most workers I met totally accept the notion that you can separate your life from your work. "No problem!" says Steve. "You just walk out that door at the end of the day and leave it all behind. Every day. Every single day I just walk away from it." Turning off feeling, closing off caring, and compartmentalizing it all certainly can't be called an optimal response. Although this is all that many people know how to do, it hardly fosters a deeply satisfying relationship to oneself, others, and life in general. Seduced by the opiate of health insurance benefits and a retirement income, workers often stay with their job many years after desiring to leave and just resentfully ride out their remaining time. Dangling on that hook, Steve swallowed the notion that he was protecting himself in the future by living a life in the present he hates.

Steve is obsessed by the feeling that he got screwed. And it's true he did, but not only by someone else. Buried too deep to talk about is the knowledge that behind all that anger about "them" and all those extra pounds of bluster hides a seething awareness that freedom is not being set out to pasture after a lifetime of avoiding thinking for yourself. For Steve, the illusion of future security has thickened into walls of his own personal prison—way too personal to talk about in some "little communication workshop" they forced him to come to.

Steve's real hunger is to be deeply related to work he cares about and that cares about him. The company he joined thirty-two years ago was all about relationships. Now it's all about control. Earlier he played the game of excellence. Now he plays the game of "how little can I do and how much can I get." Before he was happy, and now he is not. Certainly he is justified in feeling as he does. But now what? Choices of personal integrity come in the quiet of one's own conscience, except he is so filled with resentment that there is no quiet.

After class I pull Steve aside and ask if he would like to meet privately. He says he guesses it "wouldn't hurt." When we meet I ask if in his own estimation he held resentment toward the company. He nods to the obvious. I explain how such emotions are actually stored in the muscles, organs, and joints of the body and that in this way the body serves as a living, breathing mirror of one's relationship to life. I ask if he wants to carry this around with him for the rest of his days. Looking away from me in bored disgust he shakes his head no.

Sensitive to the limits of his listening, I asked if he wanted to hear more. He seemed to soften almost imperceptibly and quietly nodded yes. I said that it looked to me like he had a lot of power and strength, but he was also quite burdened. This heavy emotional weight was going to limit his expression in life until he intentionally made up his mind to let it go.

If he wanted a satisfying and fulfilling retirement he should not go into it carrying this burden of resentment. I explained how the dysfunction of the workplace worked over the years to increase his own. In continually hiding behind his justifications about management he never directly faced himself and his own contribution to the mess. This would have to be done now if he expected to be free of it in retirement.

He looked directly, and somewhat defiantly, at me while I said all this. Suddenly he looked away and let out a short breath. I paused with him. The moment grew into a very long moment. Clearly something was building within him. I let the discomfort grow. Finally in a very small voice, with eyes moistening, he looked straight at me and said, "Okay, Boss. How do I do that?"

After another long moment, I said, "That may have been the most courageous question you've asked in a very long time." He looked away from me saying, "Well, we'll see about that." I continued explaining there was an area of personal development called "deep work" that would be required. Deep work accesses new levels of vitality through looking at yourself from a much deeper perspective. It accelerates your growth and maturity dramatically, but it requires learning and stretching yourself in an unaccustomed manner.

Now, measuring each sentence, I said slowly, "Deep work facilitates the acceptance and then release of old disappointments, hurts, and feelings. Deep work means you don't keep standing pat with the same answer to life's challenges. It requires that you develop a new, more expansive vision for your future. This vision must be backed up with new practices that ingrain new behaviors. The whole process will challenge you to embody a new kind of courage. The payoff will be a tangible freedom from the past."

His big body had a visible quiver at this point. His face flushed, but he looked at me hard and straight. I looked directly back, saying, "What do you think, Steve? Are you up for it?" Walking out of the room he replied, "I'll get back to you."

The first stage of our journey together was setting up a foundation for the work. I had Steve answer questions like: *What is our purpose together? Why are we doing this? At this point in your life what is your real ambition?* From this information we formed goals that he sincerely wanted to achieve and that I knew, if he worked hard, we could deliver. This process led to Steve creating a new vision for his life, something he could enthusiastically grow into rather than just tolerate. He built a purpose for his life that set him on course to be the man he really wanted to be. I encouraged him to dream big and see himself living a life true to what he felt in his heart, a life that reflected how much he obviously cared for people. It was a vision requiring him to take different actions in life, not just have new understandings. Against the backdrop of this purpose and commitment we went to work.

Steve was a classic deer hunting and fishing type of guy, a man's man, at least in his own eyes. True to this image, he developed over the years the tendency to subtly oppose any pressure, or expectation, he felt coming at him from someone else. Naturally, then, when I would make a suggestion concerning how to handle something not working in his life, he would immediately raise his voice, get defensive, and push back. The combination of this attitude and his overbearing size was usually more than enough to make people back away. The more I pointed this out the more his sensitivity increased, yet so did his awareness. I did not ask him to change his behavior, only to notice it. Each time he reacted that way I would simply ask if he was aware of it and did he really want to be like that. At this point he would make an honest choice as to how he wanted to relate to my questions. Every time he resisted I would honor his choice and just point out what he was doing.

Time and again I made note of all the different ways he pushed back against new information. We began to connect this tendency with much larger issues in his life and see it as a very basic relationship he had to his body, and in fact to almost every thing and every one. Once he made this connection and saw the effects, he slowly began to drop his guard and voluntarily open up.

One of the first orders of business was addressing his extra weight. We did so from the standpoint of referring to it as a coating of emotional protection he had layered on himself. I told him it would naturally fall away as he allowed himself to feel more deeply, speak more honestly, and listen more compassionately. I explained that as these layers of insulation fell away it would probably leave him feeling a bit raw and vulnerable. I continued saying, "Denied and suppressed emotions resurface at these times. The trick is to move toward them, not away, and be willing to learn and grow from what you experience." It takes courage to do this, the kind of courage Steve was not used to having. He could be very brave in situations requiring a stern exterior and manly physical strength, but this deep work would require feeling his soft side, his hurt side, the part of him long since calloused over and covered up.

Our time centered around practices that would develop his mental, physical, emotional, and spiritual strength. This involved two different weeks of ten- to twelve-hour days doing everything from meditation, to working out at the gym, to deep emotional release and taking long walks together in the mountains. Key to all this, and linking it all together, was working directly with his body to access, and then release, deep patterns of unconscious experience buried within him.

We talked about how one's body naturally organizes around and reflects your experience, and that you are literally shaped by how you experience life. In other words, the shape of your physicality holds the form of your experience. Someone who is trained can see this constantly reflected in the posture, movement, breath, and general shape of any person. I called this an *embodied attitude*, meaning the way a habitual mood or a particular experience had over time embedded itself in the very shape of the person.

To deepen this understanding, I asked him to stand in front of a full-length mirror, look at the person he saw there, and tell me what general attitude this body reflected. At first he was very uncomfortable with the process and basically found it quite difficult to cooperate. However the longer he stood there the more he could actually talk about what he saw instead of just being embarrassed. During this time of looking in the mirror I asked him questions like: *What is that body trying to feel? What is that body trying not to feel? Where is energy collected and stored? Where is energy lacking? What does that shape like to encourage? What does it like to withhold?*

He sat down at one point to rest his legs and I asked him to imagine what a body would be shaped like if it were organized to "reduce excitement." In other words, how would a body be shaped if it were configured to keep excitement to a minimum? After first giving his usual "I don't know, Boss. That's what I'm paying you for" response, he named off physical traits very close to his own.

Steve was a very physical person and, although this mirror exercise was quite challenging, he became fascinated with the study of being able to see these qualities in people. He wanted to know more and more about what I saw, how I saw, and the theory behind it all. I suggested that instead of talking about the theory he actually experience it for himself.

I motioned him to lie comfortably on his back while I sat at his side. I asked him just to lie there quietly and tell me whatever he was feeling. The first stage had to do with getting past his usual round of jokes about the process being either sexual or painful. I understood his discomfort, because asking a person to lie down like this is not a normal social posture and therefore quite unfamiliar in the presence of another. In this sense it required us to move to a different level of trust together. Once he began to relax a bit I asked him to drop below the level of his thoughts and tell me what sensations were going on in his body. Where did he see them? How did he feel them? Were there any paths of sensation he could trace going from one area to another?

Once he felt secure in just being aware of his own sensations, we moved on to the next, deeper level of awareness. As he opened his eyes I asked him to take off his glasses and follow me in some eye movements. I placed my finger about twelve to fourteen inches from his face and asked him to follow with his eyes while I slowly moved it in different directions and patterns: small circles, bigger circles, figure eights, near and far, slower and faster. After a minute or two of this I simply asked him to close his eyes and tell me what he noticed.

After saying he felt strangely more relaxed and at home with himself, he again wanted to know about the theory behind all this. I explained that as his eyes relaxed so did he. I continued saying that how you see cannot be separated from you as a whole, and that vision is largely something learned, not genetically determined. As such, people have adopted visual patterns of tension and holding that reflect the same patterns in the rest of their body. I said, "Let's see if you can feel the truth of what I'm saying from inside yourself. Just lie back and relax. Let what I am about to say sink in and then see for yourself if it makes any sense. Try and hear my words not just in your mind, but from within your body."

Slowly saying each sentence and then letting it stand on its own for a moment, I said: "The eyes are part of a total system that perceives reality. The eyes are the gateway to the brain, which controls the central nervous system. How you see both affects and mirrors the condition of your nervous system. Compensations, or tension, in your vision reflect your life experience and choices you have made about how to interpret the world. The totality of these choices is an attitude, a posture and a viewpoint carried in your mind, your body, and your emotions."

We started all over again with him lying down and relaxing. I knew we would have to take this slowly, and that at each new stage he would want to step out of the experience to understand the theory behind it. This, of course, was his way of controlling the situation and making sure he didn't feel anything too far outside his comfort zone. I was fine with that, and we kept up a steady banter, joking about when he was finally going to let go and just experience it.

In the next stage we brought in breath. Drawing deeper breath into the body raises the excitement level of the whole body and tends to bring repressed emotion to the surface. In addition, when you bring your breath to particular parts of the body it brings new awareness and sensation to that area. This can also reveal where excitement and sensation are blocked. I asked Steve to begin a particular pattern of breathing and to keep it going until he felt resistance to doing it any longer. At that point he would rest and then shortly after that I would ask him to begin again. As he repeated this breathing pattern over and over the energy or "charge" in his body slowly began to increase. Each time he rested his body would be more charged with energy and I would gently touch a part of his body I knew was holding tension. At other times I would massage a very tight muscle. During other rest periods I lightly tapped an area that appeared to be numb or uninvolved.

At each stage he went deeper and deeper into himself. He seemed to feel himself from the inside as never before and was awash in a sea of sensations and feelings he had never felt before. It was both amazing and unsettling, or at least this was how I saw it. Soon he needed to open his eyes and sit up just to gain some sense of normalcy. It took a few moments for him to collect his thoughts.

He looked into my eyes more openly than I had ever seen before, saying he felt "good" but "kind of weird" and that he felt me "seeing into him" deeper than ever. I said the feeling was weird because he probably felt more naked and exposed than he was used to. At this point I talked about *armoring*. Armoring is like a shell one wraps around oneself for protection. His body showed this in many places. Armoring functions like a mask hiding essential hurts, tender feelings, and strengths. When you touch the body what gets evoked is a history, a background of memories living behind the mask. Often this in turn evokes a flood of sensations long since stored and awaiting release. These sensations carry with them a narrative or story about what we feel. As new sensations come to the surface, so do new stories or narratives.

In Steve's case these memories were of early days at the company when he was new and wanted to please by working hard and showing people he was tough. He told me story after story of times he was hurt by what people had said but could not show it. On and on he went, releasing painful memories of when he thought he could count on someone and they let him down. At the time he had neither the communication skills nor the depth of relationship with people to work it out, so he just carried this sense of betrayal around within him and continued acting cool. Afterward we had a long discussion about the fact that these memories were lodged in the tissue of his body, not just in his mind, and that we had freed them using touch and breath, not just psychology. I continued saying that when you free the body, and not just the mind, you increase the chances of a person becoming a different actor in the world, capable of taking different action and not just thinking differently.

One of Steve's main physical goals was to "lose his gut," meaning have a flatter stomach. My contention was that he would do much better to get interested in his "core strength" and take up a physical program that would train this quality. A flat stomach was a particular look he wanted. A living strength in the core of his body would bring him something much more essential. After a bit of convincing I began to teach him core strengthening exercises. To my surprise he practiced them regularly. Over the months of our working together he experienced a major reduction in back pain, neck tension, and other related problems, directly as a result of this practice.

At one point later in our process together he became furious with me about something I said. After I apologized, we both agreed his reaction was much stronger than what my words had merited. His overreaction was a predictable result from years of stored-up anger, the kind I had seen that very first day of the communication workshop. From this point on we worked out his anger energy on the heavy bag. This meant lengthy, exhausting sessions during which he would hit the bag with a bat over and over again while letting out any kind of sound or words that he felt like. I would encourage him to really go for it, even when he had nothing more to give. Each time he would reach new levels of power and intensity even though exhausted, and then he would experience release from his past pain. Increasing amounts of self-forgiveness, relaxation, and peace would flow from there. Whenever I suggested we go to the heavy bag his first reaction was "Oh no, man. I don't need that shit again!" Once we started, however, he relished the idea of aggressively and uninhibitedly beating that bag. I always made sure he understood that the point of the process was to safely release negative energy and then to make accessible more feelings and sensations.

At one point he said, "Hey, Boss. This is kind of like wringing out an old sponge, huh? It makes space for something new to be absorbed." People like Steve grow old prematurely because they stop growing and just stubbornly hang on to old habits that bring no real vitality to their mind/body system. We talked about how one of the main aspects of health is learning to get "empty" by taking appropriate actions (like hitting the heavy bag) to release old pent-up thoughts and emotions. Without this ability to release, your system begins to shut down because it is overloaded and holding too much. Once the skill of emptying is learned the system naturally can cleanse itself and be restored. This is where *practices* come in.

Practices are a way of training yourself to ingrain new, positive habits of being. To make any clear change in life, particularly one as big as what Steve was attempting, you need to adopt daily practices that will continue the process of growth and change over the long run. From the beginning, part of my deal with Steve was that no matter how good or how bad it got, he would keep going with the practices we established because they were the foundation of building who he was to become.

Steve had the most trouble with the practice of meditation. He was suspicious of "the spiritual thing" and joked I was trying and convert him with all this "brainwashing" and that my real motive was to land him in "some damn cult." Each time he brought it up I knew that although he was being funny he was still serious. At this point I would just ask him what he wanted out of his life and whether or not we were making progress on that. We agreed that "progress" meant developing a greater capacity to be his own unique self. Real progress meant that each step of the way he could, by his own measure, say he was gaining ground in his capacity to bring more focus, more relaxation, more honesty, and less defensiveness to each new moment of time. This became the criteria for what worked and what didn't.

We joked about how the heavy, withdrawn, serious part of him had given way to a natural lightness, and with it came a deeper, more heartfelt laugh. When Steve and I first met he was actually swollen with a stubborn resistance. As this quality began to subside, Steve, in his own view, became more innocent, less jaded, and funnier. During the year Steve shed layer after layer of what we called "excess baggage": negative thoughts, feelings, and pounds. Some days he felt great, other days the opposite, but always he kept up the most fundamental practice of all: honestly admitting where he was at and continuing the practices.

Each week on the phone we would talk about his life, his vitality, and his relationships. He had an increasing sense of undoing in one year what he took many years to put together. As he gained momentum he talked about how his sense of purpose in life had changed, how the energy within him had increased, and how friends remarked that he looked good. Then he would humorously tag on something about how his golf game had also improved, but I knew he was proud of his achievements.

Every once in a while Steve would get discouraged, usually because he could not tolerate some new, uncomfortable feeling. Each time this happened he would want to be reminded about "why this is worth it." Again, I simply would ask him what really mattered to him in life. Each time it would come down to family, living with a sense of vitality and purpose, and making a positive contribution to the people he cared about. Clarity about those simple desires kept him doing the practices and expressing what was truly in his heart. The more he found those truths the more his burden lifted, his vitality increased, and he gained momentum in achieving his goals.

Everyone wants to wake up in the morning and be inspired with who they are and what they have become. Steve was no different, except that when we first met he thought the way to do that was to avoid the dark places in himself. As he found out, this will just not get it done. Steve put his big shoulder against the wheel of his life and pushed himself into a new future by clearing away the negativity of his past. The more he was able to do that the more energy he had for the present and the people who were in it.

At one point toward the end he said, "You know what, Boss? When I first came to you I thought I was all broken and you were going to fix me. You didn't fix me. You showed me a whole new way of living. I wouldn't call it easier, just a lot more fun." Life's challenges go on for Steve like they do for all of us. The difference is that now he continues to grow more and more heartened by what he sees in himself.

Chapter 8

Leadership Development and Increased Productivity at Work

~ Peter Luzmore

We knew it was going to be bad news. You're never told to be at an emergency meeting to hear that a customer is delighted with your work. What made these meetings even more uncomfortable (and unproductive) was the anger and upset that came with them. We were all gathered together in the conference room when in came the senior vice president. Six-foot-six, he is imposing on a normal day, but when he has just been with a dissatisfied customer he gets really angry. His face flushes red, his look is scary, and his voice is raised. "You need to get your act together. This is not acceptable … yet another big problem with a major customer." We are told to come up with a plan to get us out of trouble. He will be back in an hour to see what we have to say for ourselves. He leaves and we all sit there stunned; not only do we have a dissatisfied customer, but we also have a livid senior vice president to contend with. We are paralyzed, with no idea of how to produce any kind of plan that doesn't pose the danger of triggering another outburst.

This incident happened five years ago. What follows is the story of this senior vice president, Pete, and how we fundamentally changed his leadership style and transformed his team from a bureaucratic culture that created resentment and resignation into one that was entrepreneurial and driven to build an organization that produces both customer and employee satisfaction.

We were in the design stage of planning a ten-month leadership and team development program. I had produced a lot of trust in my work with the executive team over the previous months, but I knew that to introduce this new somatic technology as a core component of the program was risky. I was going to have to proceed cautiously. We were not especially interested in the participants' ability to repeat back a theory, but we wanted them to be able to take action, to *do* what they had learned. Instead of having the participants read a book about leadership skills, discuss the topics raised, and watch videotapes of great leaders, we were going to have them *lead* people. We were going to put them in exercises where they experienced leading and sometimes failing to inspire a group of people. This is a much riskier proposition for the participants, because in order to learn this way you need to recognize that it is often uncomfortable to be a beginner and that messing up is part of the learning process. It is also risky for the teacher, because if you create too much discomfort, people are going to forget that they are beginners and forget why they wanted to develop this skill in the first place. Then you will have revolution on your hands, the program will get cancelled, and the previous good work will be forgotten.

This was a traditional bureaucratic work environment where some of the employees had been in the same department for more than twenty years. Additionally, quite a few had been teachers and were used to delivering traditional education. Despite all this, I felt that using traditional education methods would not be able to produce the cultural change required. We would have to design this program so that the participants experienced what it felt like to be entrepreneurial. We would have them *be* effective team members or discover what was getting in their way, and they would develop the competencies to be successful. This approach would give us the best chance by creating the momentum to start to shift this bureaucratic culture.

My first attempt focused on describing a set of exercises taken from aikido that uses a Japanese wooden staff, or *jo*. These exercises, or *kata*, are effective in the participant starting to develop an awareness of what sensations get triggered as they go through a set of thirty-one moves with their *jo*. Unfortunately, I made the beginner's mistake of describing the exercise over lunch as opposed to having the participants directly experience the sensations and thus be able to understand the relevance for themselves. There is a big difference between explaining something so that someone can understand it and having them immediately sense or feel it. It's the difference between knowing how to do something and actually doing it. When a practice is readily available or embodied, it doesn't take any thinking or mental activity—you just do and it becomes increasingly transparent as you become more competent. Pete remembers the proposal to include a *jo kata* as a practice for the team development program: "You talked about bringing in a piece of wood and doing exercises with it. I rejected that as too marginal, convinced that it would distract from the real purpose of the program."

So it was clear that I was not competent to demonstrate the possibilities of this new technology. I had the executive team spend a day with Richard Strozzi-Heckler of Strozzi Institute and thus experience for themselves what I could only describe. This produced the results I wanted. Most of the team saw the possibilities, but not all of them liked the practice or saw it as relevant. The other senior vice president of the division was very clear that this was not for him, though he would not get in the way if this was what the group wanted to do.

We set off on a ten-month leadership and team development program that included a major section focused on this new approach to enable learning. The program included a set of exercises at the four conferences, plus a daily practice. All of the exercises were designed to develop the participants' ability to observe what they were sensing. After they made such observations, we then had to teach them what to do about them. One of the fundamental competencies we taught them was to settle or *center*. When life throws you off balance, it's important first to be able to observe that, and then to settle back and center yourself so you can determine the most appropriate action to take rather than just automatically react.

One of the themes of the first conference was developing the ability to coordinate with others. The fifty participants were taught a partner centering practice. In this exercise you experience how you have different experiences when coordinating with different people and what it feels like when there is uncertainty that produces a lack of coordination (especially common when you start working with a new partner). Beginners in this exercise tend to get off balance; some pass too close to their partners, other too far away. They may go faster or slower than their partners. People have even been known to bump into each other. The exercise is a metaphor for real life. In this exercise people get to see how they react in their work life. By becoming better observers of the sensations that are created, they can then take steps to settle and become more effective at coordinating with others. During this exercise we often have the participants stop and observe the sensations that are being created as they coordinate with their colleagues. After they have developed some basic competence in moving together, observing and centering with one partner, we then expand the exercise to include twenty people. This enables the participants to see how they automatically react to situations when they could quite possibly "go into overwhelm." The coach makes observations and suggestions to the person who is moving with the twenty people. During this exercise Pete was coached to observe his tendency to collapse in on himself, head down, his shoulders hunched forward. It looked like an attempt to close people out. Pete remarked that "this coaching made a big impact on me. I saw that many times I was much more comfortable in my office with the door closed, working with my papers and doing email, rather than dealing with people and their possibilities." From another participant was this message: "Thanks for the centering practice. After some upsetting calls, it used to take me fifteen minutes to recover and get back to work. Now, using the centering practice I can recover and get back to work in three to four minutes. Thanks for those eleven minutes."

By the end of the first four-day conference everyone was excited about going back to work to apply the new learning. Shortly thereafter there was a substantial push-back against doing the assigned daily practice of five minutes of the partner centering practice. As the course designers, we knew the importance of a daily practice to the development of the participants' ability to observe the sensations triggered by daily work and life events. But, as was mentioned earlier, there is a big difference between people understanding the theory and embodying the skills so they can move into action. So even though people had repeatedly said at the conference, "Yes, I can see the importance of a daily practice and I understand the possibilities for me and my ambitions," there were a lot of complaints about actually having to practice.

In the end we came up with three alternatives: five minutes of a movement sequence we call the "two-step," five minutes of centered walking, or sitting for ten minutes. Pete remarked, "I remember being initially disappointed with the sitting practice. I had no idea of the power of the sitting practice until I really got into it." With the three options available the participants settled into their practice sessions and the resistance progressively disappeared. They saw that a daily practice would enable them to spend more of their day present, open, and connected.

Ten months later, when the program was completed, the impact report predicted that over the next three years there would be a $784,000 (375 percent) return on the investment in this team. As for this new technology, fifty-three percent liked the focus on this approach during the conferences, and sixty-three percent agreed that is contributed to their effective teamwork.

After the leadership and team development program I started on the next phase of my work with Pete. In order to have him spend more time present, open, and connected we needed to change the way he experienced the world. I had learned that we experience the world through our bodies as sensations. If there is something about the way we have configured our bodies during our upbringing that gets in the way of the flow of energy as we experience different emotions, then we will not be able to manage our emotions or moods. Configuring our bodies includes many aspects, from the way we hold our shoulders, to a leaning forward all the time, to a rigid military jaw. We can change this configuration by working directly with the body. There are many different ways to do this, including regulating the flow of breath and moving the energy so that it can once again flow through the body unhindered.

In Pete's case we needed to work on two areas: the way anger showed up, and his tendency to slip into resignation if the world wasn't going the way he expected. The goal was not to prevent him from experiencing the sensations associated with getting angry or resigned, but rather to give him a way to observe and manage the associated sensations. Over the next two years he engaged regularly in bodywork exercises, producing by his own admission a dramatic effect on his development.

Being present, open, and connected is a major part of having a life that is productive and satisfying. It can mean different things to different people. When I talked to the executive team that reports to Pete and asked them to discuss what changes they have seen, they made the following assessments:

He smiles now. When I talk to him, I feel connected. Before I would tell him about a problem and he would be off thinking about the possible solutions while I was still talking.

■ ■ ■

He has more attention on a larger worldview now, more than just the specifics. He is patient and focused on listening and then facilitating, rather than telling you the answer. It feels like we have a stronger personal connection, making eye contact and small things like saying "Thank you."

■ ■ ■

I have seen a great change in him, particularly in the way he responds to situations that in the past would have caused him to overreact. He would get angry; his face would get red and very tense. We would shy away from having any contact with him or just say something to placate him. Now there is much more calmness in his conversations as well as in the way he shows up physically. He seems much more willing to listen, to be compassionate with people. I still see him as a strong leader who has his opinions. He hasn't lost that, but now there is an interest in looking at different options and concepts in a very objective way.

Pete himself reports, "I always thought that leading was about having the right ideas. Now I realize it's more like blending with people and being the right person." The executive to whom Pete reports sees him now as a natural leader, someone he can count on to work with his peers as issues arise between them and the board.

Pete told me a story that includes an assessment from his fellow senior vice president:

A month ago we had a customer in here who was really upset, and he was blasting us, unfairly in many cases. I had all the background information and was really feeling the urge to fight back. But I didn't let that erupt and handled the person appropriately. I took care of him. I gave him some ground and blended with him. My fellow senior vice president said afterwards, "As a result of those courses you've taken, you've avoided the bloodbath that could have happened. The courses have really paid off." That says a lot about this person, as he was so opposed to this approach. I take that assessment very seriously.

This is a new technology available that can allow us to develop our leadership skills and make us more productive and satisfied with our work lives. Given that we spend so much of our lives at work and that so much of our identity is tied to the kind of work we do, it's important that we spend the maximum amount of that time present, open, and connected. Yesterday, I walked past a conference room in this organization and inside there were four people practicing their *jo kata*. To some it looks like people waving around pieces of wood; to others the participants appear as committed to a practice that will develop their ability to sense and experience life more fully.

Chapter 9

Listening to Bodies Long-Distance:
The Power and Possibility of
Telephone Coaching

~ Suzanne Zeman

I t was Thursday afternoon on a beautiful sunny day in the San Francisco Bay Area. My office phone rang and I heard the voice of John, a client in New York. He was calling from his house in Westchester to ask for help after a tough day at work. He had just started a new position as vice president and general manager of an Internet business, and there were people he was not getting along with. I could sense how anxious he was, so I asked if he was willing to do something different than we normally did.

In my years of study in somatics and my experience as an executive coach, I've seen the power of working with a person's whole being. This means I work with a person's physiology, background, mood, emotions, conversations, and spirit to enable them to take new actions. In these early sessions with John, I started experimenting with how I might bring somatic awareness to clients without their being physically present. I have found that this is not only possible, but it is also powerful for them.

On that day I asked John to describe his surroundings and what he was looking at in that moment so he could begin to locate himself in present time. He said he could see the trees blowing in the wind outside the windows of his study at home. We both stood up in our different locations and I asked him to practice centering himself, connecting to the ground by feeling his feet on the floor and then opening to the sensations in his body.

S: Let's scan through your body to see if you're holding tension anywhere, and see what we can do with that. Bring your awareness to the top of your head, then feel your skull, forehead, and the area around your eyes. What do you notice?

J: I feel pressure on the sides, around my temples, and my eyes feel a bit squeezed and hot.

S: Tell me more about those sensations. Is there a color or temperature there?

J: There's a darkness that's beginning to get lighter, and now it feels a bit cooler around my eyes. They feel softer.

S: Any thoughts?

J: I'm remembering a tough conversation I had with one of my colleagues today, the CFO [chief financial officer]. He said he was annoyed that I wasn't giving him the financials that he asked to get regular reports on. He was sharp and had an attitude that made me want to tell him where to go. If he could have waited for me to explain, I would have let him know I've been restructuring the reports so it would be easier for him to get to the numbers he wants.

S: Can you relax some of the tension around your temples and eyes? Try taking a full breath, and as you exhale, let some of that go.

J: Much better.

We continued, with me guiding his awareness through the rest of his face, neck, and shoulders, until we got to his torso. It was interesting to me that he had very little sensation in the front of his torso but felt lots of energy coming into his back. He said the energy felt strong, like a "torrent," but he stopped feeling anything when I asked him to bring his awareness from the back, through his torso to the front of his body. I asked him what he thought about that, and he said it was kind of weird, but he didn't know what to make of it.

My sense was there was a connection between the lack of feeling in the front of his torso and his communication challenges. I asked if he would be willing to try an experiment with me for the next couple of months. I would focus on helping him not only with the CFO, but also with the identity he wanted to establish in his new company. He agreed to have weekly calls with me and to do the practices that I asked him to do daily. First, we started working with his breathing.

S: Where do you feel your breath, John?

J: Kind of in the middle of my chest.

S: What about when you take a deep, full breath?

J: Well, it goes up higher.

S: Can you feel the shape of your lungsælike big pearsæfull at the bottom? Try breathing with your hand on your belly and move your hand with your breath.

J: Hey, I can feel that now!

I asked him to practice taking full breaths, moving his hand with his breath for five minutes or more each day, and note what he was feeling. At the end of the session, he said he felt refreshed and energized.

During the next session, he reported that he could relax more easily using the breathing practice. His voice was becoming more relaxed as well. He did this practice prior to his staff meetings and discovered that it was easier to be with his employees. He was much less anxious and better able to listen to them.

We increased his breathing practice until his breaths became fuller and he could feel himself breathing throughout his torso. When I asked him to move his awareness out to his skin from the inside, he was able to do that as well, and he felt the energy under his hand. He also noticed that his voice was softening and becoming more resonant. He committed to practicing breathing, relaxing, and moving his energy when he noticed any anxiety in himself or someone he was speaking with.

John told me he was much more at ease at work after doing these practices for a few weeks. He also said he wanted to become a better listener, and that he wanted people to know him in a way that was closer to the person he saw himself to be æ mindful, caring, and dedicated to the success of the business. I decided to work with him on bringing his awareness to his body and extending his energy forward to be better able to connect with people.

We began the next session with breathing, centering, and connecting with each other, I in my office, he in his. I guided him in the next steps, not sure how we could do this over the phone.

S: John, now that you can feel your breath throughout your torso, let's see how far you can extend your awareness out in front of you.

J: I don't have any idea of how to do that.

S: Okay. Try putting your hand on your belly and breathe into your hand. Good. Now what are you sensing at the interface between your breath and the container of your body?

J: Well, I feel some sensation and warmth. It's almost tingly just under my hand.

S: Imagine that the tingling sensation is brought about by lots and lots of tiny bubbles.

J: Like champagne!

S: Let those bubbles move out from the front of you and follow how far they go with your awareness.

J: I have a sense of bubbling about a foot out in front of me.

S: Now continue breathing, and with each exhalation, send more of those bubbles out from your torso. Good. Keep extending.

■ ■ ■

Energy Follows Awareness

We worked this way for the next few minutes until he had a clear sense of energy moving forward from his midsection. Using the principle that energy follows awareness, I tried an analogy (champagne bubbles) that he could understand to bring his awareness to the edge of his physical form and beyond. I noticed I could feel a shift in my own body when he was able to begin extending, producing an increased connection between us.

John's practice of extending out produced some interesting changes in how people paid attention to him. He told me that in the following week his colleagues and staff seemed to be listening more and taking what he said more seriously.

In our next session, I guided his awareness to extend his energy out from the middle of his torso, around his back, and out horizontally, until he had a sense of a sphere of energy all around him. We practiced contracting and extending the sphere until he had some control and could sense extension and contraction with his awareness.

The next step was to practice connecting with other people by extending his energy to the center of someone he was talking with. After several more sessions of practice with me and then on his own, he could tell when he was connecting and when he wasn't. He said that when he stopped to connect before listening or speaking the other person stayed right with him. Their communication was easier and more effective. When he didn't connect and wasn't conscious of extending his energy field to the other person and blending with him or her—when he was thinking about something else, for example—misunderstandings and negative emotions easily resulted.

I coached John for fifteen months as part of a program that teaches the discipline of management and leadership using somatic and linguistic practices. Regular coaching helps participants bring their learning and practices into their work and lives, learning within their daily concerns and challenges. When we started, John was resigned and blamed his bosses for not giving him direction or providing advancement. Once we worked somatically in our coaching sessions, John's progress accelerated, and he has been able to maintain his self-confidence and ambition.

■ ■ ■

The Essence of Communication: Connection

I've learned through my experience of more than twenty years in sales, management, consulting, and coaching that the essence of communication is connection. The more deeply I connect with someone, the better I'm able to hear their most fundamental concerns, their most precious commitments, what they care about, where their pain is, and what inspires them.

When working with people long-distance, I don't have visual cues to assess their shape and determine where they may be holding back or are constrained. Instead I look for other ways to help them open to increasing awareness, energy, and capacity to take new actions. I open myself to connecting through my senses. I feel their breath, hear their voices, listen to their stories, moods, and emotions, and connect with what they care about. This allows me to determine whether they are acting consistently with their concerns and designing their life in a way that is satisfying. I listen for openings to suggest new possibilities, looking for where to move with them by asking questions. In this way, listening deeply can actually be enhanced via telephone, since I don't have the visual input that might be distracting in some situations. I listen with my whole being. And then I ask questions to ensure my listening resonates with theirs.

A coach who has somatic sensibility, whether a manager or someone from outside a team, can listen deeply with their entire being. They can question, reveal, and take action to remove the hindrances to alignment among team members. This is possible over the telephone, without the traditional visual and sensual cues that we use when meeting face-to-face. The key is a strong connection between the manager/coach and team members. Then people's moods, concerns, emotions, and passions can be revealed, heard, and resolved for the future success of a project, product, or plan.

■ ■ ■

Technology: Help or Hindrance

Today's technology—including cell phones, email, and chat rooms—produces more information flow but less connection. Technology allows for quicker literal connection (we immediately find the other person or instantaneously get the memo to them), but its very speed can hinder the authentic connection of really being there with the concerns of the other. This challenge is evident in the literature on communication in virtual teams. A study done in 1997 reported that eighty percent of companies were working in virtual teams, with people in different locations, different time zones, and different cultures working together via technology to accomplish a mutual goal or project. By now that percentage is higher. What we're seeing is that technology both opens possibilities for communication and coordination and also hinders effective communication and coordination. Using technology saves the time and cost of travel to bring team members to the same location, savings that go directly to the bottom line of a business. Files, reports, memos, and meeting notes can be shared on the web so that all team members are fully informed about what other team members are doing. However, the use of technology produces more potential for miscommunication, misunderstanding, and lack of coordination when team members naturally interpret the documents, notes, and even intentions differently based on their own listening, background, and automatic interpretations. A team leader conducting a meeting over the telephone must pay attention to individual and group moods, energy, emotions, and concerns, both spoken and unspoken. If these are not taken into account, there is a high probability of misunderstanding, causing project delays and breakdowns that can easily offset the anticipated cost savings of working virtually.

■ ■ ■

Conclusions and the Future

Connection with others is either happening or it's not. When we're connected we enhance our ability to produce the results we intend. And when we're not connected, we plant the seeds for misunderstandings and breakdowns. As a coach, I produce connection and a safe environment for the people I work with. They can then open themselves to new possibilities to produce their desired results. The connection can actually be enhanced by working over the telephone, when I create a sanctuary by listening deeply with no distraction to hear emotion, pain, passion, inspiration, and joy that wants to be expressed.

By the way, another interesting change happened for John. As he practiced extending his awareness and energy further, he thought about ways to build his identity with his colleagues, both in his company and in the broader marketplace. He initiated brown bag lunch meetings in his office, during which he and his staff talked to people in other departments about the work they were doing, so there was a broader understanding of their roles. In addition, he called several trade organizations in his industry and offered to speak at conferences and be part of panel discussions. Within a few months he had lined up three speaking engagements. His self-confidence improved and his mood became much more positive as he continued generating new possibilities for his success at work and developing his identity and career.

Part Four

Taking It to Education

Chapter 10

When the Classroom Door Swings Inward

∽ Peter Reilly

It is only with the heart that one can see rightly;
what is essential is invisible to the eye.

—*Antoine de Saint-Exupéry*

It was my first year teaching English to middle school kids in a small Adirondack mountain town in upstate New York. I had begun this teaching assignment, my first, in January because the teacher who began the year had decided not to come back after the Christmas holiday. She had lost control of the class, was tormented by her students, and left in tears each day. Her advice to me, "Don't let them do this to you," fell on the youthful ears of someone who believed that such a thing could never happen to me. How wrong I was. Buoyed by their success in removing one teacher, the students set out to remove a second. Thus they began their relentless assault on me. Although things were difficult for the first few weeks, I believed I had won them over with two days of particularly great lessons. My students were not trying to disrupt me as they usually did by waving their arms to interrupt my lesson with purposefully irrelevant questions such as, "What are they serving for lunch today?" No, for several days they had been peaceful, demonstrating no disruptive behavior of any kind. I felt particularly entertaining, interesting, and informative.

As they were leaving class on the third day I felt on top of the world. What could be greater than teaching kids? This was what I envisioned teaching was all about. That's when one of the boys stopped and pointed to the classic portrait of George Washington that hung on the wall of the room. "Mr. Reilly, that's what they've been doing all week." Covering the portrait and the wall around it was a mound of white spitballs representing hundreds of clandestine shots from plastic straws. All this was done during what I thought was my best teaching. I was dumbfounded. I had grown up believing in the traditional paradigm: teaching is talking, learning is listening, and knowledge is in textbooks. I may have been teaching, but they weren't learning. I was completely disconnected from the real focus of my students, target practice.

I stood in that drafty classroom in the Adirondacks, aware that my students and I had been assembling in the same physical surroundings each day and going through the motions of education, but we were totally absent from each other. I realized that my approach to teaching, which focused almost solely on content, kept my students at a distance. When disconnected like this, I saw people as objects rather than three-dimensional human beings. Most students possess powerful radar, a kind of "pure vision" that sees through the words of the teacher to reveal the person speaking the words. When my students detected that their concerns and needs were not important to me, they reacted by letting me know that mine were not important to them. It is clear to me looking back at my spitball experience that some of us go through entire careers without ever noticing the truth of the spitball-covered portraits in our classrooms.

I needed to be more present, open, and connected to my students. Why? Because learning has its greatest success when teacher and student share a powerful connection to each other. I had to listen to the class and the individuals within it with a sensing that was intuitive, not just intellectual. When a teacher sees a class as individuals and is open to working with their needs and desires, as well as the curriculum, teaching becomes a generous interaction that grants students dignity. This connection should not be mistaken for a sentimental attachment nor a condescending empathy. Through this connection the teacher establishes a powerful narrative for learning and lays out the commitments that each has to the other. It is in this connection that students grant the teacher the trust necessary to teach.

My undergraduate preparation for teaching had been wonderful. I had learned how to develop educational units, the elements of instructional design, modern teaching methodologies, and the ethics of the profession, among many other important components necessary to succeed as a classroom teacher. I had caring and knowledgeable professors. The problem was that their emphasis was entirely in the cognitive domain; there was no focus on leadership presence, intuitive awareness, and other affective skills that are the foundation of successful classrooms. Without preparation and practice I was left on my own—as are many new teachers—to discover the importance of these invisible skills, and I struggled to develop connections with my students that would permit learning. Many teachers fail and leave the profession, as did my predecessor in the Adirondacks. Some survive by overcompensating, either straining to entertain their classes or intimidating them. Only a few learn to fully integrate their professional preparation and cognitive knowledge of subject matter with the "soft skills" necessary to connect with their students and lead their classes effectively.

What were these "soft skills" and how would I develop them? First, I needed to be much more aware of my own tendency to lose my organic connection to the class. This would require paying special attention to the signals and sensations generated within my body when interacting with my class. Second, I needed to be able to take effective action in stressful situations rather than react automatically and without thought. Finally, I needed to embody the attributes of a lifelong learner and leader.

Developing an awareness of bodily sensations was foreign to me. Generally, I tried to solve my problems by thinking them through. I could always figure out what to do to resolve things. The problem in this case was that this wasn't about employing a few new classroom management techniques. I didn't need to *do* different things. I needed to *be* different. If I had paid more attention to my bodily sensations during my spitball experience I would have noticed a vague sense of commotion when I turned my back on the class and I would have acknowledged that my students' faces were contorted in mock attention when I glanced at them. If I had effectively blended with my class I would have avoided spitballs altogether. The bodily sensations were there, but my tendency was to drown them out with my own thoughts.

Tim was a bright seventh grader with failing grades, a horrible home life, and a major chip on his shoulder. He was a disruptive kid, and I regularly assigned him to after school detention. One late afternoon with the school empty I stood in the hallway talking to a colleague while Tim sat at a desk in my room doing the reading that he had not done for homework. After twenty minutes I checked in on him to see how he was doing. I could not believe what I saw. He was holding the book upside down. Tim was being defiant even in his punishment. I felt my excitement begin to rush and strode into the classroom ready to explode in anger and establish my dominance.

For just a split second I paused and became present to what was happening. I was about to automatically explode in anger, as I usually did when a student challenged me. Did I really want to go there today? Suddenly the picture of an angry, red-faced teacher and a silly student with his book upside-down came into focus and I smiled. Immediately the anger dissipated. Tim looked up from his book with a puzzled expression, and for a brief moment we shared a transforming smile. At that moment Tim and I saw each other as people for the first time. It was extraordinary. I took the book and said, "Go home, Tim." He stood up in wonder and walked to the door. Just before leaving he turned and muttered, "Thanks, Mr. Reilly" and was gone. After that, Tim became one of my favorites and I his. Tim wasn't consistent, but there were days he would throw himself into his schoolwork or astound me with a poem. He was clearly trying to express himself. I rarely saw Tim after that year; but everything good that happened between us was the result of that pause and my conscious decision to interrupt my automatic response to Tim's defiant behavior.

When we are trained to be aware of our bodily sensations we can notice the excitement as it begins to stir and before it is so strong it launches us into the current of an automatic response. Once we are aware of the sensation beginning we can practice taking steps to regain our composure and maintaining our connection with the student. When we recenter ourselves this way we are able to take effective action on behalf of our students. I remember being horribly provoked by a student's defiant roll of the eyes in full view of my class of seventh graders. Marcy meant to embarrass me as she had on other occasions, and the bodily excitement I felt exploded in anger. Unlike during my experience with Tim, I didn't have the presence to stay calm and take skillful action. I scolded Marcy with clumsy words that flowed out of me uncontrollably. Not only did I lose my fundamental connection to her for the remainder of that year, but several years later she appeared in my class again and it was clear that she had not forgotten the incident.

I needed to learn to interact with my students in ways that were just right for the moment. One of my favorite quotes on the topic has been on my computer screensaver for some time: "working with someone where they are ... without the hindrance of a prepared sermon." It is taken from Richard Strozzi-Heckler's book *Holding the Center*. In it he tells the story of working with an emotionally disturbed teenager with a very violent bent. When asked what he would like to learn, the teenager replied, "kill someone." Most of us would have been triggered by that statement and shifted into an angry response to the words rather than maintaining our focus on the child. Strozzi-Heckler replied, "I'll show you that ... it's easy." Thus began his teaching relationship with the student. The starting point for learning is never the needs of the teacher but those of the student.

Focusing on the needs of students requires many approaches. Our modern classrooms present teachers with more challenges than at any time in the past. If only every student were willing to reveal themselves and their ambitions so that their teachers could move with them in ways that took care of their needs. Today's classrooms are filled with students who have no idea why they are there. Some of them are in temporary or permanent states of resignation or anger and push away what they desire to bring close. When we react to these moods without maintaining a balanced presence we lose our ability to find the student beneath the mood, and therefore cannot take effective action. Keeping or regaining one's presence in the midst of assaults on one's subject matter, role, or personal traits is an important component of successful teaching.

Finding students amidst the resignation and anger they can exude may require a teacher to create breakdowns or crises to disrupt the status quo. Both inside and outside the classroom, growth often follows great catharsis. Teachers who develop a strong connection with their students can sense the need for dramatic intervention and the students' ability to handle it. They also realize that there is a real commitment to the student in creating such a breakdown. Most people avoid creating these incidents because they involve an enormous amount of energy. Sometimes it is much easier to ignore a problem and continue the status quo. A breakdown event is effective only when created by teachers who are aware of their own tendencies and have a commitment to a sustained effort with a student to create a new future. Outstanding teachers often deliver great lessons in powerful ways.

In addition to working with students in the class as individuals, teachers with an effective classroom presence also sense the class as a whole. They sense the mood of the class. In order to learn the class must be in a mood of curiosity, wonder, or ambition. If the class is resentful or resigned the teacher knows that his actions and the narratives he creates around learning can shift the overall mood. For most of us the idea of creating or shifting moods is not commonsensical. We generally experience a mood as something that overcomes us. We are in it, and it has us. Being able to manage the mood of a class while maintaining a deep connection to the individuals within it is an important competency for teachers. One does not develop this competency through cognitive learning. It is an attribute that comes with practice and by developing a more present, open, and connected self.

The process of educating our children is just as important as the outcome. Most of the artifacts of today's curriculum will look strangely irrelevant when viewed in the rearview mirror of the future. I remember when, early in my career, I paused at the desk of Kerri, a shy and lovely seventh-grade girl who had written an essay about her favorite pet. I leaned over her desk and began to point out grammatical and structural errors in her writing. My finger pointed to an error in her work and next to it a tear fell, smearing the ink. Before I understood what had happened another tear fell, and then another. Kerri had written about the death of her dog and how much she missed him and I had not noticed. In my mind content had always been king. I suddenly became aware that there were larger human issues afoot in the little world of my classroom, things that mattered much more than grammar. As a teacher I held a larger place than I realized in the lives of my students. Whether I wanted the responsibility or not, I was the living curriculum.

Powerful teachers embody learning. We have compassion for the difficulties that accompany new learning because we never relinquish our role as learners. As model learners we exhibit curiosity and persistence. We take risks and, most importantly, we occasionally fail. We can relax into the uncomfortable zone of the beginner. As self-aware teachers with strong connections to our students we never hide our humanness but celebrate its self-generative yearnings and frailties. A teacher who embodies learning lights a difficult path that students will want to follow.

It should come as no surprise that teachers must maintain their mastery of subject matter and that students must show levels of achievement and learning that meet federal, state, and local standards. Developing our bodily awareness, intuition, and leadership presence does not require giving up our existing competence. When we blend our existing subject matter mastery with the ability to connect with our students, act skillfully in difficult situations, and embody learning, we sharply increase our effectiveness. The beauty of developing teachers who embody this holistic skill set is that we can enhance our ability to meet our curriculum objectives, as well as provide our children with models of adult behavior. We can do this without adding another "thing" to the classroom, but by rediscovering the wisdom that lives within us, and living in ways that turn promise into practice.

Ask successful veteran teachers about these invisible classroom skills and they will acknowledge that they exist and reinforce how critical they are. They will talk with pride about the important lessons they have learned throughout their careers about classroom connections and leadership presence. It is sad that all this hard-won knowledge disappears with each teacher's retirement. Given the importance of these skills it is surprising that there has been no national movement to teach these skills in any systematic way.

Every undergraduate program that prepares teachers should provide its students with curricula that reveal these new distinctions. These programs should provide the extensive practice necessary to have these skills embodied and at hand when needed. Programs that develop the leadership skills and presence of corporate executives and managers are common throughout the private sector. We can do no less for our teachers. We should commit ourselves as a nation to the proposition that every teacher will enter the classroom with the rich palette of traditional, professional skills that have been provided for decades; but they should also be prepared to lead their students by connecting to their needs, working with them where they are, taking effective action in stressful situations, and exhibiting all the excitement and uncertainty that comes with being a learner. By developing teacher preparation and professional development curricula that focus on blending cognitive skills with embodied leadership presence, we can greatly increase the retention rate of new teachers, improve the performance of veterans, and provide a much more meaningful learning experience for our students.

The real promise of creating a generation of teachers who employ body, mind, and spirit in their teaching is that millions of students who may have dropped out, either formally or informally, will stay engaged with learning. We will ensure the equilibrium between compassion and rigor in our classrooms. We will not sacrifice learning in order to develop self-esteem, but neither will we ignore the needs of our students in the process of learning. All this can lead to a generation of present, open, and connected students that listen deeply to the concerns of others and embody what it means to be lifelong learners. Able to pause and be fully present rather than thrown into automatic responses that limit their possibilities, our children will create new futures for themselves, and in the process lead us competently, deep into the twenty-first century.

Chapter 11

The Embodied Writer:
The Flesh into Word
∼ Mary Michael Wagner

Our most sacred convictions
Are judgments of our muscles …
Perhaps the entire evolution of the spirit
Is the question of the body.

—Nietzsche

Moment by moment,
things are losing their hardness;
now even my body lets the light through.

—Virginia Woolf

In the 1940s, the University of Iowa established the first creative writing program in the United States. Today, more than three hundred colleges and universities offer such programs. Before this innovation, writers studied technical writing, grammar and rhetoric, and, of course, literature. But with these new programs, writers could actually apprentice to become poets, fiction–writers, and playwrights. They could study how to create fleshed-out characters and craft strongly plotted stories, how to write sestinas and haiku; they could have their work critiqued and learn to effectively revise it. In short, writers could practice their craft.

What the university discourse doesn't address, however, is the underbelly of writing. How does the writer face the white page? How does he or she tolerate and even thrive from critiques? It's widely agreed that writing takes a certain amount of courage. Cynthia Ozick claims, "If we had to say what writing is, we would define it essentially as an act of courage." She admits, "I have to talk myself into bravery with every sentence." Having taught creative writing for seven years, I have observed that without these skills, even a vastly talented writer will not succeed. But if the writer doesn't have these non-craft-related skills innately, how does he or she cultivate them?

Somatic practices can be used to address challenges such as resistance to writing and the anxiety of having one's work critiqued. They can also simply harness greater potential: although the body often seems wholly missing from the creative writing discourse, deeply inhabiting the body in fact means gaining a fluency in both sensation and emotion that can infuse one's writing with a greater sensuality and depth.

■ ■ ■

The Dive into the Body

Last night a noise woke me. In moments I was out of bed, poised at the front door, phone in hand, index finger on the number nine, the other hand resting on the doorknob. I blinked back into the darkness of the house. Hazy thoughts, like the contrails of an airplane, trailed seconds behind my actions. The back door's been opened. Someone's in the house. The bathroom window's shattered.

My thinking self soon discerned that a ceramic pot had turned over in the wind and shattered on the back patio; but it was my *body*—the sound traveling into my ear canal, spawning a rush of chemicals out into my limbs—that had set me in motion. As I stood at the door listening back into the stillness of the house, my heart felt engorged and a pulse whomped in my throat. A ropy, liquid feel, a watery shakiness, gushed and spread into my arms and legs.

The basic texture of our inner lives depends to a huge extent on the constant flow of signals from the body. According to brain researcher Antonio Damasio, people with "locked-in syndrome," a type of paralysis so complete that those afflicted can communicate only through subtle eye movements, report a surprising lack of terror about their condition. The reason, Damasio says, is that such people have no way of using the body as a "theater for emotional realization."

For the rest of us, in moments of extremity, we meet our bodies. In an interview Alan Ball, screenwriter of the film *American Beauty*, recalls, as a high school student, being in a car accident in which his sister died. He describes "a moment, a very distinct *physical* sensation of the bottom dropping out."

For a writer, being able to inhabit and render these pinnacle moments is essential. To discern gut reactions in charged moments is easy, but what about this powerfully nuanced physical system in less charged situations? What does it feel like moments *before* we fall in love? Or what does sorrow feel like in the body—not at the funeral, but three weeks afterward? What does the small happiness of seeing snow falling in a field feel like? These aren't so clear. And yet we live our lives in the smaller, more sublime moments. A writer must be able to render viscerally not only the climax of the story but also the slow, incremental ratcheting up of emotion and action.

In the smaller gradations of these responses to less earthshaking life events, what signals do our bodies slough off into our nervous systems? What warnings or pleasures? The man on the street who stopped to pet my dog a few weeks ago did not set off the visceral, gut-twisting response I felt hearing the pot crash in the middle of the night. Here is only a guy in a red cable sweater stopping to pat the head of a scraggly-haired mutt. We have greeted each other. He is squatting beside me. I stare off over the top of his head toward the row of new stores at the bottom of the hill, telling myself not to forget to get milk again. As the guy scratches my dog's ears, I am silently chanting *milk*, imagining myself in the dairy aisle. I am also trailing somewhere behind myself—fuming over a check the bank is holding. I'm everywhere but in the present moment.

Rubbing my dog's head, the guy says the dog's name over and over: "Buddy, Buddy, Buddy, Buddy." Then he slowly tilts his head up at me. "Which house is yours?"

A heat shimmies into my chest. I notice that the fur on my little terrier's neck is ruffled. He already knows that if this guy isn't dangerous, he's a creep. What if I had been awake when he approached? What might I have noticed; what signals might my senses have wicked up? How his sweater reeked of mothballs, how he swiveled his head to see if anyone else was around? What sensations might the radar center of my body have been sending out—a slight shivery feeling in my chest, diaphragm muscles cinching themselves a notch tighter?

In this situation, I certainly would have been safer had I been more aware. But as a writer, what price do I pay for being asleep? Of course, human beings drift off, become unmoored, daydream. But how much of people and sensation rushes past me in those moments when I seem to have vacated my body? And why is that important?

■ ■ ■

Openness and Sensual Detail

As a writer, I feel called to be aware of the happenings inside the whirl of my body and mind and emotions; and perhaps what these things point to—though I am unsure—is my soul. Just as vitally, I must try in a piercing way to understand and deeply see these things in other human beings. This is what being awake means. For writers, this carries an extra challenge, for by necessity we are careful observers, and observing can easily lead to a remove. I remember a radio interview in which a writer described being present at the birth of his first child, the most important, most potent moment of his life. With an undercurrent of sadness, he recalled that his writer self pulled slightly back, recording, watching. If this is inevitable, one can counteract by being an active observer—not just eyeballs staring out at the world, but instead an observer who is deeply attached, deeply acting from the heart and the viscera. I actually envision roots traveling from my eyes down to the bloody, pumping sac of my heart and the gnarl of my guts and into the muscles and tissue of my body. I try to build the practice of allowing what I take in through my eyes to impact me. Chögyam Trungpa Rinpoche puts it this way: "If you put your hand through your rib cage and feel for it, there is nothing there but tenderness. You feel sore and soft. … It occurs because your heart is completely open, exposed. It is the pure raw heart. Even if a mosquito lands on it, you feel so touched." This is what it means to be an embodied writer.

Through our bodies, we interface with the world. Through our bodies, the sensual raw material of the world enters us. Diane Ackerman states that "there is no way in which to understand the world without first detecting it through the radar-net of our senses." Australian director John Duigan opens his film *Flirting* with a voice-over passage: "I remember the smells most: stale lockers with fruit cakes rotting into the wood, crusty shoe polish, damp towels, quick ink for fountain pens, disinfectant on the floors of the shower block, fresh chalk, moldy oranges blue with mildew, and on a rainy day, the deep, rank, wild smell of discarded football boots." His ability to soak up these sensory details and then, later, translate them into language grounds the viewer in the world of that aging boarding school. This sensual grounding is the most basic and most potent ingredient in writing; it allows the reader to viscerally inhabit a world.

By makeup I am a frenetic person. The motion has kept things at bay in me. Growing up, I gravitated toward sports, activities that involved speed and motion. The practice of somatics—of consciously experiencing breath and subtle movements—has slowed me down. Through this slowing down and expanding of awareness, I can note more of the sensual information that enters me and then in turn utilize it in my fiction. If a writer is skillful and particular enough, the reader can be impaled on the sharpness of the story details. William Blake maintains, "Singular and particular detail is the foundation of the sublime."

■ ■ ■

Rendering Emotional Complexity

In the beginning, my writing was like a giant eye observing, chronicling. My characters had no internal lives, no emotional lives. Even a first-person narrator—often chosen in order to reveal a complex interior—for me was only a roving eye that watched. It paralleled my life—I was often more observer than participant.

I remember skiing all day as a kid, even though my toes would freeze. I couldn't bear to come inside before I had to. When my mom pulled off my boots, I would sob and hold my frozen toes in a puddle of warm water in the sink. A terrible prickly feeling much worse than the cold numbness would enter the soles of my feet. Learning to reinhabit my body wasn't so different.

I used to barely breathe into my chest. My somatic coach spent months helping me relearn to take in a full breath. I had learned to hold my breath in fearful childhood situations, and years later I was still holding it. My body had shaped itself around that habit, the muscles holding my chest down, holding back sensation and life. All the tiny muscles around my ribs, the gnarl of tendons and ligaments, had to learn to move again—a slow, excruciating process.

But as I began to take in more air, my muscles softened. Also, my feelings thawed. As my body woke up, my writing began to deepen and my characters took on greater depth and nuance and emotionality, greater complexity. I was able to imagine viscerally what it felt like for a girl to be called a woman: *A little current of feeling goes down my back, like something being unzipped, at being called a woman.* I could describe the *physical* sensation of complex feelings: *Already there was a sort of tenderness forming in my throat, the beginning of a secret.* I knew what grief *felt* like: *Everything was raw. As if our plumbing had been removed and replaced with smaller veins and arteries and colon, so that our blood, our pumping effluvia, had to overnight squeeze through impossibly tight places.*

■ ■ ■

Kate: Creating a Focused Narrative

Kate's stories were wild and messy, thickets of startling imagery and quirky characters. Although her work was imaginative and compelling, reading it was like being blasted by a tsunami—no handholds or path, only onslaught. And as much as she tried to write a focused, cohesive story, the main plot line petered out into a gnarl of tangents.

A kind of energy radiated off Kate, as if her head were a hive and energy zinged around it like buzzing bees. In conversation, she would start sentences she didn't finish and tell three stories at once, sometimes breaking into unexpected laughing jags. All her liveliness seemed stored in her expressive face. Her lower body—especially her legs—seemed lifeless, inert.

As Kate began doing simple movement and breathing exercises, that buzzing current began to filter down from her head and into her torso. Holding her arm, I could feel coursing energy like water gushing through a garden hose. Here was a person who had tremendous power, if only she could harness it.

As the streaming built and radiated down through Kate's torso, she reported feeling overwhelmed. What became evident was that the energy wasn't reaching her lower body. When standing, Kate locked her knees and pelvis. This locking served as a dam, blocking off the stream of energy.

No wonder the sensation that built up in her upper body was so overwhelming that she felt compelled to discharge it continuously in chatter and sudden, disconnected bursts of laughter. Just as TNT is compressed into a small chamber to make it explosive, all of Kate's energy was packed into her upper body.

Using hands-on work, I worked first to create less contraction in the muscles of Kate's lower body, softening the locking and holding in her knees and hips. Between sessions, Kate went on long walks and used weight machines where her legs could push and lift; this brought strength and aliveness into her lower body. As energy began to move throughout her *entire* body, it felt more diffuse, less charged. The built-up pressure dissipated. The ricocheting, uncontrollable thoughts and tangents gave way to a steadiness. Her legs served as grounding rods, helping conduct the intense energy down throughout her body, instead of being lodged in her head and upper torso. This grounding translated into her fictive worlds as well. Kate became able to refuse the pull of tangents and instead to sustain gripping, focused plot trajectories. Her stories had a beginning, middle, and end now, and a palpable rising action.

■ ■ ■

Marvin: Overcoming Resistance

Knowing is not enough; we must apply. Willing
is not enough; we must do.

—Goethe

It's the first day of the semester: new notebooks, stacks of shiny-covered books, young writers on the edge of their destinies. At the end of class, after students have discussed their deep longing to write, I always ask, "Who feels resistant to sitting down and writing?" Almost the entire room of arms goes zinging up into the air like hopeful antennae.

This has been the central dilemma of the writers I have known. It is not desire and longing—not even a startling literary talent—that will determine whether these writers find their way into print. The single biggest indicator will be whether they can get, as Mary Heaton Vorse says, the "seat of the pants to the seat of the chair."

Volumes have been written about how exacting writing can be. Gene Fowler wryly noted, "Writing is easy: All you do is sit staring at a blank sheet of paper until drops of blood form on your forehead." If you search the Internet, you will see thousands of pages on writers and procrastination. Ralph Keyes, in *The Courage to Write*, a book devoted solely to that topic, describes E. B. White as "a gifted procrastinator" who "by writing long letters and puttering about his farm … often managed to avoid the trauma of writing altogether." So, it takes courage, chutzpa, whatever you call it, to face the empty page. But how does one summon this courage?

Last year, I began working with Marvin, a young "thwarted writer," as he called himself. He possessed an amazing raw talent that had frequently been recognized and awarded when he was in college, but writing had since turned into an excruciating stop-and-start process for him. Marvin's writing mind was never turned off; he would show up at sessions with words penned on his hand from ideas that had materialized while he was on the bus. Once, the writing trailed clear up to his elbow. But when Marvin actually sat down to write, he would find himself organizing his books instead—alphabetically, or in sections, and once even by height. He would bounce a ball made of rubber bands off the wall by his desk, where an observer could make out faint, smudgy skid marks. What he felt even worse about was that after that caginess evaporated, he'd secretly lie on the couch and watch soap operas in the afternoon (his writing time). A feeling of indifference would overcome him, a malaise so thick that he imagined if there were a fire, he might not bother to get up.

When I was a kid, the whole neighborhood used to take a shortcut through a corner of my yard, wearing away a muddy, rutted path. Habits are like that: they become the path of least resistance. After a time, it becomes almost impossible *not* to keep going there, the habits are so ingrained and intractable. Living in those two extremes—ricocheting from frenetic activity (frantic organizing) to terrible lethargy (lying on the couch soap watching)—had shaped Marvin, built up a calcified habit inside him. When he sat down at his desk, these habits would irresistibly take over. Imagine knocking over a line of dominoes and trying to get them to stop falling midstream. That's how hard it is to change a habit.

Working in his writing space, Marvin and I began to uncover the way he moved into this cycle and to plan ways to intervene. Big and easygoing, Marvin was the kind of guy you'd describe as a "gentle giant" or someone who "wouldn't hurt a flea." Yet I was surprised at the change that came over him when he thought about sitting down to write. He would begin swaying slightly, clenching and unclenching his hands. Critical thoughts would arise inside him: "Who do you think you are, wanting to write?"

When I asked him to sink into his bodily sensations and feelings, there would be a moment when he took in a breath and reported a hot, searing feeling in his center that he wanted to get away from. He would do this by pulling away from his sensations, and moving up into his thoughts. There he would be left to marinate in his inner criticisms: not only was he "an asshole who *thought* he could write," but now he was "a writer who wasn't even writing."

During this process, Marvin's breath would become shallow and his shoulders would rise startlingly. He looked like the cliché of a henpecked husband. Here was where the collapse happened. Here was where he wanted to give up. Unable to contact that inner energy, he couldn't gain access to the stamina and drive he needed to move past his doubts. Every time Marvin sat down to write, he faced this epic internal battle. This was the portal into our work.

We practiced over and over the moment of him sitting down to write. He reported a sense of rage, a feeling as if he had swallowed burning coals. When the sense of agitation rose, he would automatically begin to tamp down on his feelings by breathing shallowly and scrunching his shoulders up toward his ears, bringing all of his attention up into his head, and into his self-critical thoughts.

After a few weeks, I asked, "What if instead of trying to clamp down on these angry feelings, you just let them go?"

He stopped pacing, his voice losing volume, the breath not even visible in his chest cavity. "I'm afraid someone will get hurt," he said.

Marvin took a step backward, creating more of a buffer between us. I noticed that my heartbeat had quickened. Here, truly, was access to something different from Marvin's "teddy bear" image. His cinching down had made him look as if he were permanently ducking, but now he stood fully in his tall frame, strong-jawed and rippling with power.

"What if what you're feeling now," I asked, "is the juice, blood, current that is part of what runs your creativity? What if you've been shutting *that* down?"

We set up an exercise in which Marvin could let this emotion move through him. With a simple martial arts elbow strike that engaged his whole body, he struck pads, using his voice with each strike. Initially, holding the bags, I felt a moment of uncertainty about what might happen. With each subsequent round, his voice came from a deeper place, as if he were dropping into deeper and deeper chambers inside. What came out, though unbound and wild, also came out directly on center, in a power harnessed and focused—not unlike the way writing can focus the creative muck inside.

Afterward, Marvin's shoulders were dropped and his breath was down deep in his belly. His jaw was softened. When I asked him how he felt, he said, "Alive."

When I asked him about the critical voices, he reported that in the first raw moments after the physicality, they were blessedly gone. Now he could hear them again, but they had less traction. They were more like hovering gnats than barbs that were able to enter him. The place in his torso where he felt as if he'd swallowed hot coals still had a sense of roiling and energy, but it felt less dangerous. He was less afraid of it and more curious about how his creativity might arise from there.

Over the weeks, we repeated this exercise before he sat down to write until the charge slowly leached out. There was almost a sense of Drano-ing out the pipes of a kind of emotional buildup or backlog. We then worked on subtler practices using voice and movement, both to expel pent-up anxiety and restlessness and to tap into that force in the center of his body.

Marvin visualized himself as having broken open the casing of a hard seed that had been lodged in his gut like a bullet. Now there was some-thing there that was not walled off, but more like an underground spring he could dip into. A writer must learn to navigate and ultimately harness this nexus of intense emotions or she will never get the seat of her pants into the chair.

■ ■ ■

The Writer in the World

When a business or restaurant tanks, it is often described in dry, tepid terms, whereas the world gives failed art a more severe public drubbing. Consider Roger Ebert's new book *I Hated, Hated, HATED This Movie*, in which he recommends that one movie be "cut up to provide free ukulele picks for the poor." I know of students who gave up writing altogether because of a single wilting remark received in a creative writing workshop. For an artist, the failure of creativity, the failure of imagination, somehow seems like a naked failure of the self.

How do writers (often utter introverts) navigate the tide of feedback on their work? Having attended countless literary readings, I've noticed brittleness in many writers. They often possess a closed body structure—folded arms, concave chests, bowed heads—a shielding stance designed to keep things out. Unwittingly, I adopted this same stance.

As a twenty-five-year-old writer, out of the blue, I received a letter from Doubleday informing me that my first published short story had won an O. Henry Award and would appear alongside the work of such writers as Joyce Carol Oates and Cynthia Ozick. I should have felt elated, but I felt nauseated. My roommate slid the letter from my hand as I crouched on the floor, hugging my shins with my arms. Success exerts its own pressure. My first story went on to win a Pushcart Prize and was anthologized numerous other times. Although I continued to write, it would be ten years before I submitted stories for publication. To inquiries from agents and magazine editors, I simply didn't respond. My aversion to the feelings of exposure simply won out over my desire to be a writer in the world.

No amount of *understanding* my tentativeness was enough. Only through somatic practices was I ultimately able to shift. I literally had to change the way I *physiologically* responded to attention and feedback. Through exercises in which I practiced being gently, then vigorously, grabbed, I learned the mechanics of what I did when I felt overwhelmed. When the world came at me, an intense heat shimmered through my chest. To lessen the sensation, I shallowed my breathing and rounded my shoulders, making my chest concave, and I often covered my torso with my arms; in short, I shielded myself. A shield might seem like the perfect solution, but it is designed to keep *everything* out. A writer wants to develop the tolerance to take in and experience *every* sensation, feeling, and thought.

In the same way an athlete trains, I practiced building a tolerance for the powerful feelings coursing through me. I shifted my sense of myself from a suit of armor with a hard casing to a skyscraper, whose strength comes from the internal girder, a strong inner core.

An envelope dropping into my mail slot still sets my heart thunking. Sensation begins radiating through my chest. Locked in that envelope is praise or criticism or indifference. As if the force of gravity were overcoming me, I feel my body wanting to fold up. But now my training takes over. I fill my chest with breath. I feel the whole slop and mess of emotion flooding me, and I turn to meet it.

■ ■ ■

The Embodied Writer

Of all the artistic disciplines, writing has the least obvious connection with the body. Sculpting, painting, and the theater presuppose a visceral quality or dependence. Words, however, are assumed to germinate in the factory of the brain and chug out of the writer's hand as if on a conveyer belt. But unless the brain is vigorously rooted in sensuality and emotion, writing tends to shallowness or flatness, a great emptiness.

John Gardner claims that a writer "labors at the very lip of the volcano." If writers are to descend into the most charged human territories, such as desire, loss, and death, they must inhabit their deepest somatic capacities. Being immersed in a culture that continually supports numbing escapism and consumerism creates an even more profound pressure for us as writers to reveal the human beings we are and the beings we might become. And since dominant media such as television, video, and film are more apt to show the surfaces of things, writing has an even stronger mandate to render the human interior. On September 12, 2001, in a piece in the London *Guardian,* Ian McEwan was already trying to make sense of the shattering experience of the previous day:

> This is the nature of empathy, to think oneself into the minds of others. These are the mechanics of compassion: you are under the bedclothes, unable to sleep, and you are crouching in the brushed-steel lavatory at the rear of the plane, whispering a final message to your loved one. There is only that one thing to say, and you say it. All else is pointless. ... You go back to your seat. 23C. Here is your seat belt. There is the magazine you were reading before it all began. Imagining what it is like to be someone other than yourself is at the core of our humanity. It is the essence of compassion, and it is the beginning of morality.

For writers, deeply inhabiting our own bodies, our own sensations and feelings, makes it much more possible that we will in a credible way take that startling leap into inhabiting the experience of another. And maybe, as writers at this time, this is one of the most profound leaps we can take.

Chapter 12

The Somatic Engineer

~ Peter Denning, Ph.D.

E ngineers are widely seen as people of great technical prowess but who are difficult to get along with, aloof from their customers, and inclined to substitute technologies of personal interest for technologies that would bring value to their customers. This exacts a huge price: unreliable technology, waste in technology development, and a standoffish reputation for all engineers. These problems would largely disappear if engineers were educated in value dynamics, the value-generating and value-delivery skills that are the foundation of leadership. Value skills cannot be learned from a book. They are most effectively learned through coached somatic practice.

I came to this conclusion by a roundabout route inspired by seemingly mundane but nonetheless important concerns of my computer science and engineering students. Students often seek help in their professional lives outside their courses. The most common complaints, especially among students holding down part- or full-time jobs, are that they feel overwhelmed, unable to fulfill all their commitments, and severely stressed in work, family, and health. Those who have been out in the field for a few years voice additional complaints. Some have great ideas but cannot get them across. Some are passed over for promotions or turned down for new jobs. Some can't believe that customers would rather use a product inferior to theirs. Some are infuriated by the shameful way companies treat them in the name of "better customer service through information technology." Some find "genuine professionals," who take care of them expertly and unpretentiously, frustratingly rare in a world dense with professionals. Many think their managers are jerks, notwithstanding the diplomas on their walls from well-known management schools. Many also think their teammates and their customers are jerks. They all think that something important was missing from their education.

All of these challenges concern *value*: the value of one's ideas, the value of professional identity, the value of results delivered on time, the value of a company's customers, the value of working relationships. My students think their education made them great technicians but did not teach them to be value-delivering professionals.

A solution to this problem with great potential is to provide value training within an engineering curriculum. Until recently I did not think it was the business of engineering schools to do this. I changed my mind when I realized that breakdowns around software quality, software safety, and software development are taking a costly toll on society and the engineering professions.

Beginning in the early 1990s, I developed courses in value training for engineers. I soon discovered that somatic learning is the key to success. This means that the training must encompass the whole body, including energy, emotions, moods, experience, cultural history, habits, tendencies, and practices. The skills and practices of value production are not conceptual. They involve listening, relating interpersonally, acting decisively, and adding value.

■ ■ ■

Sense 21

At George Mason University I called my course Sense 21, short for "Designing a New Engineering Common Sense for the 21st Century." In my first offering, I taught engineering students foundational principles of action in language I had learned from Dr. Fernando Flores. I promised to show them how to be "observers of the observers" they are. I taught the students that their life stories (autobiographies) revealed how they were shaped and how they observed the world. I taught them the importance of speech acts such as assertions, assessments, declarations, requests, and promises, and how those speech acts alter their worlds. I showed them that habituated tendencies in their bodies often prevented them from being effective with these acts (for example, when they tensed up during a negotiation, held back on an important request, or were wishy-washy about a critical deadline). I taught them new interpretations of learning, education, career, work, and innovation. They learned about the many changing roles of customers and performers. They also learned that their ability to inspire trust depended on managing their commitments well. We practiced listening to people not just as individuals but also as members of communities. And then we learned how to design engineering systems that would be welcomed as innovations in their communities.

It was a big surprise to me early in my teaching of Sense 21 that, although the students eagerly embraced these ideas, they were unable to *perform* them effectively. No amount of talk and careful explanation helped them perform better. So I had to learn coaching. I created practices that revealed their performance-blocking habituated tendencies, which I then called "thrown-ness," and I created practices that taught them effective performance. I was constantly helping students overcome their "blindness," showing them what I could see about them but they couldn't see and couldn't see that they couldn't see. Let me share two cases of how this worked.

■ ■ ■

Michael

In a moment of frustration, Michael sent me an email demanding to use a workstation in my lab to do a project for another class. I told him I could not do that because the workstations were reserved for the students working on research projects in my lab. Infuriated, he told me that I was not exemplifying my own ideal of helping students get their work done. Fortuitously, in the previous class I had discussed seduction and listening for concerns. I asked Michael if he would agree to a coaching session in class to help him get to the bottom of why he was being ineffective seducing me to his request. He agreed.

In class, I explained to the others that Michael and I were going to have a coaching session to demonstrate what I mean by seduction and listening for concerns. I asked Michael to read his email aloud and then repeat his request. Michael did so enthusiastically and quickly fell into the confrontational mood of his email. He tried half a dozen different arguments on me, all variations on the theme that I was acting unethically or irrationally in denying his request. None moved me; I declined all his requests. Soon the entire class was offering suggestions to Michael. Nothing worked. After about ten minutes, Michael was sweaty and stiff, his breath short and labored. I could sense that the entire class shared Michael's mounting frustration. I let this go on until he could take it no longer. He hissed, "Are you just playing with me? Saying no just for spite? If not, what's wrong with my request? It's perfectly reasonable!" I replied, "You have not addressed any of my concerns." With utter frustration, he threw his hands into the air, rolled his eyes to the heavens, and exclaimed, "But I don't even know what you are concerned about!" I smiled at him, leaned forward, and said, "Exactly."

Suddenly, Michael was convulsed with a Great Aha! Turning bright red he plunked down in his chair, saying, "Geez, now I get what you mean by seduction." The other members of the class looked startled and got it too. Then they excitedly urged him on: "Ask him what he is concerned about!" This he did. Soon he proposed to fashion his project to help contribute to the goals of the lab. I was seduced. We closed a deal.

I used two somatic methods in this session. First, I wanted to reveal to Michael and his classmates that he (and they) did not know how to listen for concerns. Michael was aware of his own desires, but not of mine. He was not curious in the slightest about my own interests or the history of my lab. His habituated tendency had him so busy offering reasons and logic that he could not listen. Second, I wanted Michael and his classmates to directly experience the breakdown as a biological event—through physical signs such as sweating and short breath, emotional signs such as frustration, and mood signs such as resignation. After this session I gave Michael a breathing practice to help him learn to be a better listener by watching his own energy, aliveness, and sensations as a prerequisite to becoming aware of these things in others. I also gave him a conversational practice of displaying a genuine curiosity about whom he was talking to.

■ ■ ■

David

David had received a major promotion at work. He found himself in a much bigger world, one in which he had to provide direction for many projects around the company. Now he had to rely on project managers to keep their promises, and he could no longer fall back on his old way of jumping in to rescue a slipped deadline or failing project. But he kept locking horns with his new boss in disagreements about project management strategy. He feared that these disagreements could eventually lead to his demise. One day his boss told him that he was being condescending with another member of his group. This assessment so shocked him that he came to me for coaching.

I asked David to reenact the interaction with his group member so that I could see what he was doing to provoke his boss's assessment. It soon became apparent that when a skeptic challenged his authoritative statements, David tensed up, squinted, drew his head back, and looked down his nose at the skeptic. He provoked in me exactly the reaction that his boss reported. I told him this and showed him exactly how he was provoking the reaction. He was amazed that he was doing all this and wanted to learn new ways. He saw that this would not be easy because his old habit was so automatic that it was invisible to him.

I knew from previous conversations that David was very smart and had a tendency to let things slide until the last minute, when, with his innate skill and talents, he could "pull it out." Physically a big man, he had learned to use his size to intimidate, getting others to back off a criticism or to submit to his control. I told him that these tendencies left me with an assessment of him as a cowboy, someone likely to shoot up the saloon to get his way. David's cowboy tendency was a context for his interactions with his new teammates. When they challenged him, he reacted with condescension. Therefore, I wanted to work on both these tendencies together.

The first thing I wanted David to learn was that his boss's assessment was not a statement of permanent truth about him. It was an assessment based on his own actions. He was fortunate in having a boss willing to share such assessments. I believed David could enlist his boss to help him see in real time exactly how he provoked the assessments he wanted to change. I asked him to write this down: "My boss says I am condescending. This is an assessment. I do not accept this assessment as a permanent characterization of me. I can change it. I know that I am making moves that provoke him and other people to assess me as condescending. But I do not see what those moves are. Therefore I need to find a teacher who can see the moves and give me practices to retrain myself in different moves. My boss would be an excellent teacher." I asked him to read this aloud to himself once a day for the next week, reflect on it, and learn to say it on his own. The next time I saw him, he reported with obvious delight that his boss had agreed to be his teacher. The second thing I wanted David to learn was new practices to replace the ones judged by others as condescending. I gave him practices to train humility, wonder, and gratitude. These included imitating his young son's wondrous curiosity about life and people and concluding his day by speaking or writing his gratitude for all that had been given to him that day. A few weeks later David told me his boss and his teammates now accept him as a full member of the team and that he welcomes his boss's feedback about his interactions with others.

Throughout the course I use somatic practices to train components of value dynamics. A somatic practice typically consists of two or more people engaged in prescribed movements and conversations, followed by the sharing of assessments about each other during the exercise. Many exercises are repeated with different partners. Examples are autobiography, centering, extending, blending, grounding assessments, requesting, declining, completing a workflow loop, adding value, and producing an innovation. More details are given in the figure 4. The main purposes of each somatic practice are, first, to reveal to my students otherwise invisible aspects of themselves and their habituated tendencies and, second, to connect their inability to perform these actions with their inability to produce value for other people. The emphasis is always on *how* we do something, because understanding *how* we do it gives us the opportunity to change.

Figure 4. Example Components of a Value Dynamics Curriculum

Value Component	What Is to Be Revealed	Somatic Practices
Writing autobiography	Your life is a story and you are the author	Write a story about yourself emphasizing events that shaped you emotionally and professionally
Speaking autobiography	Your comportment, posture, shape, and mannerisms reflect your history	Speak your story to a group, then receive their assessments about congruence between story and your mannerisms and comportment
Centering	You can enter a state of balanced awareness of yourself and others, prepared for action	Role playing in which you are off center in various ways; partner speaks assessments of your presence and openness
Extending	You can focus your attention in ways that command others' attention and move them to action	Immovable arm exercise; walking with intention exercise through partner barrier

Figure 4. Example Components of a Value Dynamics Curriculum *(continued)*

Value Component	What Is to Be Revealed	Somatic Practices
Blending	You are more effective if you combine your energy with the challenger's, instead of opposing or evading it	Moving toward someone advancing toward you, turning to flow with their momentum, interpreting in conversational space
Distinguishing assertions from assessments	Assertions are true or false; assessments are judgments and evaluations	Describe a table full of objects without giving any assessments. Identify assessments and assertions in newspaper articles; which sells papers better?
Grounding an assessment	People will follow if you lead with grounded assessments; most of us are inept at grounding assessments	Presenting to group "I am competent at X," then receiving their feedback
Receiving a negative assessment	You have a tendency to accept the assessment and act on it uncritically	Group forms circle, gives negative assessments to one member; recipient notices body reaction, repeats a short script to distance from the assessment with dignity
Making a request	In asking someone to perform an action for you, you provoke body reactions in that person and yourself	Make requests of partner with complete and incomplete conditions of satisfaction; trade assessments at end
Declining a request	Body reactions interfere with your ability to say no	One person repeatedly makes a request in various ways, the other declines; trade assessments at end
Completing a workflow loop	Incomplete transactions leave both parties unsatisfied and unsettled	Practice loops, breaking at each of the four stages; trade assessments at end
Trust	Keeping promises builds trust; breaking promises builds distrust	Journal of kept and unkept promises and assessments provoked in others
Mental models are distinct from practices	Knowing a concept or principle does not enable you to act effectively	Group and partner discussion of relation between theory of value components and ability to perform as demonstrated in prior exercises

Value Component	What Is to Be Revealed	Somatic Practices
Mood	Mood is a pervasive interpretation about future possibilities	Role playing with the other person posing as someone you want to make a request of or close a deal with; others observe your shape and make assessments about your mood. Practice saying characteristic conversations of various moods
Adding value	Value is an assessment by a customer	Make an offer to partner; ask what partner is concerned about, then make a new offer; compare assessments before and after
Creating waste	Actions that do not add value are waste	Role playing in which one partner performs actions that the other did not request or care about; trade assessments at end
Producing an innovation	Innovation is a change of practices in a community	Carry out a carefully structured project to design and deliver an innovation for a customer's group.

I hope it is clear that these value skills cannot be taught from a book. They are not engineering "methods" or "processes." To drive this point home with my students, I repeatedly demonstrated to them that a clear conceptual explanation of a value skill was of almost no help to them in actually performing that skill competently.

In the end, value dynamics enabled my students to listen to customers, formulate offers that would bring value to them, manage their commitments, and deliver the value promised. When combined with their engineering, the value training enabled them to be designers of innovations, an important engineering skill. (In value dynamics, we define an innovation as a new practice that the group found more valuable than a previous practice.) Master software designer Bert Keely of Microsoft told me recently that the Sense 21 principles of design teach exactly the design practices he's used for years; the Sense 21 articulation helped increase his own awareness of how he designs.

The Sense 21 project has been a phenomenal success. Nearly all the students thought this was the most important and valuable course they had ever had, and some even called it "life altering." The graduates of the original class formed an alumni group, which they called Sense 21, so that they could continue to meet and discuss their ongoing learning. Later graduates also joined. The group is still active today, ten years after it started. Sense 21 demonstrated that engineering combined with somatic practices that engage the whole self through physical, linguistic, and social awareness is more powerful, and valuable, than engineering alone.

■ ■ ■

A Personal Note

From the beginning, my heart has gone out to students who came to me for help with breakdowns they were experiencing in their personal and professional lives. Like Peanut's Lucy, I sat behind my desk listening to my students and dispensing logical, rational, and intellectual advice. Because I had become an expert at containing my emotional rushes and reactions, I was almost completely unaware of my own body, my own sensations, and my own flows of energy. I could not empathize with other people's emotions because I did not sense them in myself. My logical advice probably rang hollow to many of my students because I did not address how they were feeling and experiencing. When I became a manager I was very competent at the management processes of stating our mission, defining our promises, recruiting good people, and getting things done on time. But when a disagreement came up in the group, or a confrontation, or anger, or even great joy, I would pull back from it. If someone confronted me, I would tense up and defend. Some of my teams became dysfunctional because I was unable to move with the emotions and moods of the group.

Dr. Fernando Flores's language-action principles made the first real dent in this. He showed me that I was not a skilled performer of basic speech acts and that my fears of negative assessments and emotions kept me from successfully accomplishing the simplest of things such as making or declining a request. But I found it frustrating that my knowledge of such a powerful framework did not help me in challenging or charged situations, where it mattered the most.

The addition of somatic principles to the language-action framework made a dramatic difference for me, and then for my students. I finally learned to sense my own body and to release the old contractions that contained my emotional energy. The more I became aware of my own sensations, the more I was able to be aware with others. I began to experience genuine connections with other people and to find that I could listen for what they cared about. Once aware of what they cared about, I more easily formulated actions that were of great value to them. I came to see that many of my colleagues in computer science and engineering were in the same boat I was. We have all been trained to deal with abstract concepts, not with sensing, living bodies. Most of the breakdowns that our users experience with software and computers would be avoided if software engineers knew how to listen to their customers. I see that all I have learned in Sense 21 and from my teachers can now be synthesized as value dynamics and can help them. I am working with national and international curriculum groups toward adding a value dimension to engineering education.

Chapter 13

Somatics and Parenting

~ Karen Short

As a parenting coach I seek to encourage somatic awareness in the vocation of parenting. Although the continuation of our species may depend on our ability to birth and raise children, I believe the quality and success of our society is a direct reflection of our competence and attention to parenting children. If we strive to increase our parenting skills we need look no further than ourselves. What I've come to discover is that encased within our body lies a compass that guides us and can be accessed through the process of somatic awareness. Observing and interacting with our children through this new awareness will lead to changes in our parenting relationship. If one is willing to be guided by the unconventional forces of sensations, mood, and energy, then the journey of parenting can become one of the richest and most rewarding experiences of your life.

Many parents seek to do more than simply raise their child. They are actively involved in their child's life and strive to be an influence in the shaping of their child, aware of the power they wield as parents. Consciously parenting children is a process of creating philosophies, intentions, and practices that are unique and specific to each family. When these components of conscious parenting are in alignment, capable children are produced and harmony within a family is promoted. When something falls out of alignment the harmony of the family is disrupted. If this alignment is not restored, a gap can develop in the relationship between child and parent that, if left unattended, widens over time.

The challenge for many parents is that their daily practices are sometimes inconsistent with their objectives or intentions. They unconsciously lean on ineffective or unexamined habits. Some of these habits may be an echo from their own childhood or routines they created when their child was younger and had different needs. Parents cannot understand why they continue to struggle and, as they look outside themselves and their practices for answers, they may begin to create an inaccurate perception of their child. As the habitual cycle continues this perception becomes predetermined and evolves into a characterization for both parent and child.

To understand the impact of our perceptions in parenting we must understand that perception influences attitude, motivation, and behavior. A child's self-perception is generated as a result of the conclusions they come to about their experiences over time. If we keep them trapped in our inaccurate perception and create reinforcing experiences in their life then they may surrender and embody our perception. Both parent and child continue to act out of their perceptions, perpetuating the cycle of struggle.

It is possible to develop a parent's ability to see that somewhere between the stimulus of their child's behavior and their automatic response lies a moment where they can choose their actions and break the cycle. The ability to see that there is a choice is achieved through somatic awareness. Dr. Richard Strozzi-Heckler refers to our body becoming the source of information in his book *The Anatomy of Change*. He writes, "In the art and science of somatics, we are encouraged to become the source of our information by participating in our knowing and self-discovery. We become the source by contacting our body. In doing so, we bring to light the dimensions of gesture, stance, attitude, emotion, and that which is the foundation of all life, energy." Discovering how this awareness influences our perceptions and actions is fundamental to the process of change. When we experience connecting with our children through somatic awareness we tap into our inner compass, a source of wisdom that, when combined with practical knowledge, guides us to making the most effective, respectful, and compassionate parenting decisions. By becoming aware and available to make conscious choices in our parenting we create the opportunity to produce harmony in our families.

We become the source of change by bringing attention to the sensations and feelings in our body that create our perceptions of the world. Developing a competency in somatic awareness will allow us to utilize these sensations as the source of our information and enable us to create or choose our responses. As a parenting coach my objective is for parents to become self-sufficient in producing a state that is referred to in the somatic discourse as "centered." When parents are able to relate to their child from their "center" they have more patience and flexibility and are able to make conscious decisions as they parent their child, even in the midst of chaos.

Dr. Strozzi-Heckler further defines center as "a state of unity in which effective action, emotional balance, mental alertness, and spiritual vision are in harmonious balance." In our journey to becoming centered we look to our body. We explore nature's version of the vertical, balanced, relaxed, and open alignment of our body and we bring our attention to the center or core of the body, just below the belly button. As we begin to realign our body we may experience sensations of discomfort or awkwardness, and we may feel an urge to adjust back to our "normal" state. By repeatedly bringing our attention to this realignment we are practicing to discover "center" within ourselves.

We awaken the observer by becoming aware of the sensations in our body. We are looking to identify places of tension, pulsations, temperature, pain, aching, or twitching. We scan our body to feel where we are constricted or holding our muscles tightly; here we are looking for clenched teeth, squinting eyes, pursed lips, tense shoulders, a holding of the breath, a constricted abdomen, a sunken chest, and any other areas where our muscles are rigidly holding an unnatural shape.

When we explore our sensations and constrictions we begin to become aware of "the foundation of all life, energy." As we practice gently tightening and releasing the muscles of our body we begin to experience the sensation of generating energy. We connect to our child through the extension of our energy; and when this originates from our center it is experienced as love, compassion, understanding, and leadership.

Occasionally we experience bodily sensations that cause us to invent an interpretation that explains or justifies a change in our somatic state. These interpretations are neither true nor false but rather stories we invent that shape our perception, and ultimately our response, to the world around us. For example, does the clenched jaw tell us we are angry; does holding our breath reveal that we are in fear; is the sunken chest a way we keep from getting our feelings hurt; and are the tight shoulders left over from the days when we had to defend ourselves against attack? When we use our somatic awareness to slow down this process of creating interpretations we are then able to see the possibility for intervening and inventing new stories and perceptions that are consistent with our concerns.

If parents are to be able to utilize somatic awareness in their parenting they must first accept that they are beginners. Being a beginner means that we have compassion for our learning process, are gentle with ourselves when we make a mistake, and commit to learning. In order to embody our learning we must invent a recurrent practice. In the case of somatic awareness we practice bringing our attention to the sensations in the body, we locate our breath and energy, and we check in with what interpretations might be forming. Through this practice we will develop competency in somatic awareness and become better parents.

Experiencing our energy from center may arouse compassion and purpose that leads us to seek connection. We begin to look at the people around us with new eyes and consciously expand our somatic awareness to include observing others, especially our children. Remaining centered within our own body we see that we are separate from our child and that there are now two sets of concerns. If we are successful in expanding our sphere of awareness to include our child we can then begin to extend our center and blend with our child's concerns. Once a shared center is achieved we, as parents, can then lead our child and coinvent.

Creating a sense of balance and harmony in our relationship with our child, we extend further to include the family unit. As we become more connected to our centered presence we may tap into a sense of purpose or meaning in our life that we then include in our expanded sphere of awareness.

The following examples illustrate the use of somatic awareness in parenting situations and demonstrate how this awareness can help guide us to choices in parenting.

One of my clients, John, came to me because his son was refusing to go to school and he was concerned that there was something more to this situation. John explained the many different approaches he had tried, all of which had failed to resolve the problem. In our discussion John began to realize that he blamed his son for being irresponsible and not applying himself. When I asked John to tell me three things that his son was doing well in this situation he was stumped. I began to suspect that John had lost connection with his son and was now acting blindly out of his perception. With the intention to shift John's perception of his son I asked John to observe his son closely for the next week and write down two things each day that he appreciated or admired about his son. During our next conversation John shared with me an experience that helped him realize he was not connecting with his son.

One day a friend stopped by to visit. I excused myself for a moment as she and my son began to talk. The topic of school came up just as I was re-entering the room and I stopped at the doorway to pay attention to their conversation. As she spoke to him I noticed two things. First was the reaction from my son; her words were like a horse whisperer calling out his essence. I saw how his eyes became wide and welcoming, his muscles relaxed, as he leaned toward her. He was fully engaged with permission to be who he was; it was as if he finally found someone who spoke his language. The second thing I noticed was that she used all those phrases I had read about in the parenting books and appeared to mean them. When she asked him "How did that feel?" she embodied care and concern, her musculature was relaxed, and there was gentleness in her voice. She didn't assume to know how he felt, and his words hit her body as if they were the first time she had ever heard them. Her eyebrows were raised, her mouth was frowning somewhat, and her body was slightly collapsed, as if she had been pushed in the chest. As he told his story she seemed to be able to feel the same sensations he felt. She did not sit in front of him with authority and expertise but was rather open to being informed by him as she listened to him deeply. She spoke to him from a place that conveyed to him: "I care, I feel your upset, and I too see your concern. Judgment, advice, lectures, and morals didn't exist between them. I hadn't realized how hurt he was and how badly he felt about himself. I began to wonder how much I don't know about him and how he might guide me to help him, if I would just listen.

In this example we can see how acting solely from our perceptions we lose connection with our children as well as the wisdom they have to offer. We see that a centered presence can extend out and contact our child, and if that presence is met and accepted by our child, a connection is formed. From this connection we can then lead and influence our child. A child's essence is revealed in this sacred moment of connection, and almost magically everyone is speaking the same language. Trust and safety are produced in this connection, and everyone involved is willing to open up and become more vulnerable. Where there is no fear of being judged there is a willingness to risk oneself, and it is in this open state that true communication occurs.

Like John, Sharon has already realized that she wanted to be able to create a centered connection with her daughter. Through our work together she is becoming more observant, but this "somatic awareness" remains only an interesting concept to her and she has yet to discover how it could help her in her struggles with her daughter. We continue to look to the sensations, mood, and energy of her body for answers. In our next conversation Sharon shares with me a passage from her journal that tells a story of her somatic awakening and how her child guided her there.

A quick wave of guilt hit me and my protective fortress of blindness was beginning to crumble. I caught a glimpse of myself in a mirror and saw the scowl on my face, the tightness in my jaw, and hatred in my eyes; it frightened me. When I next encountered my daughter in her room I put my hand on her back. I could feel the tightness in her muscles and the slight pull away from me. My heart sank. There was still the coldness in her eyes, what I could see of them, as she refused to look directly at me. Her shields were up and they were strong. I was ready to kiss and make up but she was not. Her rejection hurt me even more, and I could feel the anger and blame rise up in me, only this time I was paying attention. There was great wisdom in her to keep a safe distance. Shelly was speaking volumes without a word and I could now "hear" everything. I feared doing more damage, so I said, "Well, I see you want to be alone," and walked out of her room. I took a couple of deep breaths (as deep as they could go in my constricted chest). I considered how I could speak in "I" messages and I tried to distract myself with the dishes, but I was still aware of the overwhelming feeling of wanting to keep control.

I could no longer ignore the tightness in my chest and arms, the way I was holding my breath, and the clenched jaw. In my heart was unconditional love, but the muscles of my body held anger and revenge. My body was like a well-trained fighter in the area of protecting my pride, every muscle sculpted to perfection at holding in anger, righteousness, and resentment in the face of fear and failure. I was eating away at my daughter's sense of dignity to feed the hunger for my own. It was a bitter-tasting pill of awareness. I was beginning to distinguish my own feelings from those of my daughter.

Feeling a bit desperate to release some of the tension in my body, I headed to the privacy of the garage. I vigorously jogged in place until I couldn't continue; I pulled out the hand weights, exhaling strongly with every motion. Finally I could feel my arms loosen, my chest relaxed to accommodate the deeper breaths now required. My eyes and jaw gave way only slightly as I laughed at how ridiculous I must look right now. The more physically relaxed I was the more in control I felt—in control of myself, that is. My image of Shelly changed from opponent to child, and I now found myself curious to understand what was going on with her.

In this example Sharon begins to see herself somatically. She notices sensation, energy, and interpretations being formed. She observes her child's energetic withdrawal that has resulted from her previous reactions, yet she does not judge her child. Although she begins to change her perception of the situation she notices that her somatic presence is still incongruent with her intentions by her daughter's reaction and refusal to connect and make up. Children are somatically aware and are observing us as well. This mother demonstrates the value and possibility that exists in staying connected to the practice of somatic awareness. When she notices the somatic incongruence, revealed by her daughter, she makes a conscious choice to shift her body. Many times we change our body to fit a situation, but this mother makes her shift by working with the body. When she begins to release some of the physical holding in her body her perception of her child changes and she begins to make different choices. The mother consciously begins to create an alignment between her intentions and her somatic presence. Note that the depth and impact of this experience is not in a linguistic world but in a somatic world; what happens between this mother and child is energetic.

Sandy and I have been working together to improve her parenting skills, and she has become more aware of her somatic presence. Here Sandy not only practices defusing a situation in her home, but she also starts to teach her child somatic skills and opens the space for a discussion that allows for learning.

It is time for showers in the Jensen family. Eight-year-old Ann falls off the sofa to the floor "Ohh," she wails. Her father, busy reading his newspaper, is irritated, shouting "Ann, I don't want to deal with this every time you have to take a shower!" Ann's mother, Sandy, is in the other room reviewing her mail and is grateful that she is not in the middle of the shower discussion. As she glances through the doorway she notices Ann on the floor. Ann is on the edge of a meltdown, yet she appears to be trying to hold it together. Her hands cover her reddened face as she fights back the tears. Her body is struggling to contain itself, and something tells Sandy that this is no ordinary meltdown.

Sandy enters the room and kneels to be close to Ann. "What's going on?" she says, truly curious. The Jensen family has been practicing conversations about feelings and moods, so this is somewhat safe territory. For Ann the answer comes quickly and like a flood. "I'm just having a bad day. First I woke up cranky, and I was up all night because I had a bad dream, and we were almost late for school, and the kids at school were kinda mean." Ann continues to relay the pain of her day and how the kids at school, including her best friend, found the game of throwing a ball at her head funny. For Ann the pain of betrayal by her best friend is almost unbearable. Ann's father and brother, who were also listening, offer their advice. They talk about finding the courage to stand up to bullies, or walking away, or finding other friends. Even throwing the ball back at them is considered, and Ann blurts, "If I did that I wouldn't have any friends … you just don't understand." Ann falls back into a mood of frustration as her body tightens into a hard shell, she crosses her arms and clenches her jaw, and glares at her brother.

Sandy feels ready to rip the eyes out of the children at school and she wants to lecture her child about true friendship, but in this moment she knows that this won't help. Ann couldn't hear anything, as upset as she was at that moment, and Sandy knew it. "How about a bubble bath?"

Sandy suggested. "It always makes me feel better." "No, I just want to take a shower and be done with it," Ann snaps back, committed to staying upset. Sandy gently nudges forward, "Well, it's up to you. We could make a special bubble bath and listen to some music to see if it could change how you feel, or if you want to take a shower that's fine. Just let me know." Now she is holding Ann in her lap and gives her a hug. She whispers into Ann's ear, "Sometimes hugs work to change moods too." Sandy can feel Ann holding her breath and says, "Breathing works too." As Ann took a deep breath her tears started to flow and Sandy playfully added, "Crying also works." Ann burst out half laughing and half crying.

Together they went upstairs and drew a warm bath. As Ann soaked in her bubble bath listening to gentle music and sipping on an iced lemonade she and Sandy shared openly about the importance of relationships, developing friendships, and the closeness they felt for each other in the moment. In the end they agreed that bubble baths really do help to wash away bad days.

This story demonstrates the value of extending somatic awareness beyond oneself. Here Sandy demonstrates a competence in somatic awareness with her initial assessment of the situation. Sandy's husband has misinterpreted the situation; he thinks this is a temper tantrum about taking a shower. Sandy connects with her daughter by getting physically close to her. Building on earlier family practices, Sandy creates a connection and a safe place for her child. When Ann reveals herself and becomes vulnerable, her father and brother, acting out of good intentions but not fully observing Ann, offer advice. Ann is not open to advice and it falls on deaf ears. Amidst the upset within the family Sandy maintains a centered presence by staying in touch with her somatic awareness. She chooses to attend to Ann's needs despite an impulse to respond differently and is able to extend her sphere of awareness to include her daughter. Sandy maintains a centered somatic presence and doesn't rush, allowing Ann to experience the full upset of her emotions. Sandy then helps her daughter to regain center by teaching practices with the breath that lead to a physical release.

Not only do Sandy and Ann experience a rich and rewarding bond, but Sandy also helps Ann become more somatically aware and competent.

These parents and others have taken on the challenge to become better parents. They have done so by understanding the influence they have in their child's life and examining their habitual style of parenting. By facing their perceptions of their child they become open to seeing the world differently, and as they develop a somatic awareness through sensations, mood, and energy, they begin to make different choices. Becoming somatically aware does not guarantee the elimination of all parenting problems and challenges. It is, however, the foundation for building and maintaining a healthy, dignified, and respectful relationship. This chapter is not about becoming a perfect parent; it is about becoming human with our children. Children awaken and respond to a sincere and embodied presence, and parents discover there is joy in parenting. If we are human we celebrate our virtues, embrace our frailties, and accept ourselves the way we are. Look your child in the eyes the next time you're with her; look deeply with curiosity and see what is revealed for you. In the end it is all about love.

Part Five

The Healing Path

Chapter 14

Building a Better Deathbed

∼ Patrick Clary, M.D.

I am a family doctor by training, with additional certification in hospice and palliative medicine. My work has never been more meaningful to me than now. Part of this comes from the sense of proportion the disaster of September 11, 2001, has given me. Although three thousand people died suddenly that day, on every ordinary day six or seven thousand people die in this country. Ninety percent of that number die predictably rather than suddenly. For most of this vast majority, death could occur at home surrounded by family, in comfort, with appropriate support. This is what polls and studies say most Americans want at the end of their lives. Instead, more than three-quarters of us die in institutions. Half of those who die in hospitals and eighty percent who die in nursing homes die in pain. This is worse than a national disaster; it is something like an ongoing, if unintentional, holocaust, suffered in silence and isolation by more than two million Americans every year.

The suffering is unintentional only in the sense that it was never deliberately planned. But if physicians are not trained to care for the dying in this country, how can they be expected to do it well? When surveyed in 1998, only four of the 126 medical schools in the United States required courses to develop this skill. This is a culture in which death is seen as failure, and our medical schools do not train for failure but for success. Most of the dying are either neglected or abused—neglected by being warehoused more or less invisibly in nursing homes, or abused by futile treatment in hospitals. Terminal illness is the most common cause of bankruptcy. It disrupts lives in many other ways: spouses end productive careers; children drop out of school; savings and intended legacies disappear. Even death rates themselves increase—as much as tenfold among partners in the year following bereavement.

Hospice work is undeniably difficult. You lose every patient. Most are referred very late in the course of their illnesses. As many as a quarter die within a week of referral, and half get hospice care for less than a month. Hospice benefits are designed to cover the last six months of life, but often we are called in only at the end, when symptoms are too dramatic to be mistaken for anything but the active approach of death and family support systems are maximally stressed. Those of us who have done this work for a while have had a chance to observe a phenomenon we call the "hospice honeymoon": a medical, nursing, or social work professional joins a hospice agency, absolutely "gets" what the work is about, and quits after six months.

A Quaker, I was drafted in 1968 as a conscientious objector willing to wear a uniform. In sixteen weeks I was trained as an Army medic. I spent a year with U.S. infantry units in South Vietnam, arriving around the time of Hamburger Hill and leaving after the invasion of Cambodia. It was always surprising to me during that time how close living was to dying, how in the middle of a firefight the red ants kept marching down the trail beside my nose. If I shifted uneasily and provoked them, their pincers burned just as much as if there weren't death in every AK-47 round flying overhead.

In my brigade's area of Vietnam most infantry operations were in small units, platoons and smaller. I remember one morning when my platoon took up an ambush position in coffee plantations outside Xuan Loc while another platoon swept through the lowlands toward us. I had never liked the other platoon's leader much. His style was too casual for a first tour. He marched right between two radiomen, often close enough to chat with his platoon's medic, Specialist-5 Larsen, the senior corpsman in our company.

From our blocking position in ambush among the coffee bushes my platoon heard the firefight three or four kilometers away get off to a bad start. Shuddering rocket-propelled grenade explosions were followed by the sharp, separate cracks of Kalashnikovs, all before any responding M-16 fire. The platoon leader was on the radio in moments calling for a medical evacuation by helicopter. Then he called me, asking for advice. The Vietnamese had already fled and he had three wounded men, among them the medic. Larsen had been shot several times through the face. According to the platoon leader's description he was clearly drowning in his own blood. I struggled with the idea of guiding the lieutenant long-distance through a cricothyroidotomy, a technique for opening an airway that is less risky than a conventional tracheotomy. I had never done one myself and had only seen the training film. I might have tried it myself had I been there instead of at the end of a radio net. I thought the risk too great to guide a green lieutenant through it by radio. There are a lot of big arteries in the human neck. I hoped Larsen would live until the dust off got there, but he did not. I had been in-country three months and was from that day the senior surviving medic in my company. Since there was only one medic for every platoon I found myself wondering who would care for me when I got zapped: when, not if, as the casualty rate among infantry medics in my battalion was 200 percent annually.

Although I survived my Vietnam tour unexpectedly intact, this question again became prominent for me in hospice work. Care at the end of life is so bad, and I knew that I would need such care eventually. I went through a near-death experience of my own, and I found teachers who connected me more securely to my own mortal body—the body not as an academic study in anatomy, but as a living process that defined who I was. I began a daily meditation practice in which the most consistent distraction was a small voice telling me to do more hospice work. But I understood that simply doing more hospice work wasn't going to help me when my time came. What I needed was to teach others how to do this work before I needed it. Ira Byock, author of a wonderful book on this subject called *Dying Well*, is fond of telling audiences of clinicians that we are building the bed we are going to die in. I needed to help start building a better deathbed, simply as a matter of self-care.

Of course, there was a problem with this idea. I have long thought of myself as one of the shy persons Garrison Keillor describes, someone who fears public speaking more than death. Much more. I never slept the night before saying a few words to introduce a speaker at my hospital's education program. Hours in front of audiences of physicians—more often than not hostile audiences who didn't want to hear what I had to say about the inadequacies of end-of-life medical care—simply wouldn't be tolerable. I wasn't, in any event, confident that I had anything to teach. I offered my services on a volunteer basis at the best hospice in New Hampshire. Clinical practice confirmed the need to break down the barriers between my own mind and body and to bring them into alignment. As I enter the chaos of a late hospice referral I consciously center myself. The process is similar to the centering practices I learned in meditation and in martial arts disciplines.

As I began teaching from my own growing experience I began to understand that to teach something about working with the dying I needed to learn something about living the life of my own body. There were observations from others that I seemed uninterested, arrogant, disconnected, and distant. I was able to hear this criticism as helpful and took some actions to correct both reality and perception. This wasn't simply to be a change of mind but a shifting of how I was in my body.

Though I had moved to the East Coast from the west more than half a lifetime ago, I still complained that the skies out here were not big enough, not what I was used to in Montana. I began studying with Richard Strozzi-Heckler, who watched my slouching, self-effacing posture for the first day of one of his courses and made some suggestions. He suggested that I open my eyes wider, and that I take a walk through Cambridge with my head over my shoulders and my hips over my feet. I was amazed and grateful to find the same sky here as in the Bitterroot Valley.

After experiencing the difference that a simple shift to a centered posture could make in my attitude toward the world, I began trying it in my work. I found my shoulders are the most expressive part of my body when I am not centered. My posture—what some of my teachers have called my "conditioned tendency"—is a kind of apology for existing, shoulders tensely held up almost to my ears in an eloquent shrug. It also occurred to me that my apologizing shoulders held up that high also kept me from listening.

I learned to arrive at a venue some time before I am to teach and to sit quietly for a time in the classroom. It becomes a familiar place if I can be there mindfully and notice what I feel. I feel where my shoulders are and usually, in spite of all my preparation, find them up around my ears. I consciously let them down, so that my arms are hanging loosely, as if they were the arms of a coat on a hanger. Mindfulness itself is simply shorthand for the process of noting what is there, being present for it, admitting a loss of concentration, getting beyond that, and refocusing. I do not pretend to have remarkable powers of concentration, or a particularly long attention span, but the effect of this process is the same as if I were remarkable. Even a few moments to center myself can be very helpful.

If I am not able to visit the room before beginning to teach, I will take a moment in silence before I begin teaching. Silence is an old friend from Quaker practice, and it gives me a chance to become centered in the room, to let my shoulders down, to open my ears. It also seems helpful for most audiences. The sound of a Tibetan singing bowl I carry with me can have the same effect, orienting me and my listeners in the manner of cetaceans. My intention is to change the shapes of the bodies, which changes the mood.

Other measures for helping the audience center can also be helpful. I try to warn participants of what's coming. It is so difficult—and, oddly, foreign—to hear a talk about the clinical and emotional reality of death that it seems useful to have a place for eyes to rest. A dozen yellow roses in a clear glass vase on a green tablecloth are a favorite focal point, off to my left—the heart side, I remind myself. In different versions of the language of flowers, yellow roses symbolize friendship or treason. The relationship between intimacy and betrayal is important in end-of-life care, and I often use the roses to remind me to discuss this as well as to serve as an illustration.

When actually speaking I pay attention to keeping my eyes open, my head over my shoulders, shoulders over my hips, and hips over my feet. As in mindfulness exercises of other kinds, what is important is not staying centered but returning to center quickly after losing focus. I focus on the audience as human beings who are doing the best they can and who want to know what I have to teach, and I include all in my gaze.

Centering is not simply physical, of course. My first professional training was in poetry, and I abandoned a promising career as a poet on the advice of Roland Flint, my poetry mentor, when I was admitted to medical school. Work on finding my center fifteen years after med school led me back to writing again simply because I don't sing, dance, or play an instrument: poetry is my only real gift. I use my own work and others' as illustrations in my teaching. Because much of what I teach about taking care of the dying has to do with truly making contact with them—a somatic, felt, energetic presence—this style of illustration is more internally consistent than the use of PowerPoint slides in darkened rooms.

I face audiences weekly, sometimes several times weekly, and have spoken to thousands of professionals as well as many laypeople. I wouldn't claim success in the work of building the bed I will die in, although things have changed as I have taken up the work. The number of patients cared for in my hospice has doubled, and the quality of the work we do has improved measurably. The vice president of one of the local hospitals told me that she thinks I have made a difference in the quality of end-of-life care in our region. I am not confident of that. I understand that physician behavior is very hard to change. As in other situations, it is true that if a heavy object is teetering on the edge of a cliff, a mere breath may be enough to push it over.

Research in changing physician behavior suggests that there are only a few ways to move them to the brink of change. Reinforcing the behavior of thought leaders is one method. Although those of us struggling with the issue call this "preaching to the choir" with some resignation, we do note that the congregation is listening when the choir sings. Another way to change physician behavior is teach a subject you know that a clinical situation will reinforce, and then return a few months later and teach the subject again. Somatics inform us that recurrent practice is the path to redeeming our humanness—in life and death. Finally, perhaps the most powerful method for changing physicians' behavior is to change patient expectations. I try to use all of these methods: cultivating the choir, making a regular circuit of a limited number of hospitals, meeting with doctors individually, making myself available to the media, teaching in the community, and maintaining my centering practice. Of course, with baby boomers facing the deaths of their parents and thus beginning to be able to imagine their own, I may be riding the wave of a larger social movement. I know a better deathbed is under construction, at the very least.

Chapter 15

Coming Home to the Body: A Journey for Adolescents

~ Denise Benson

High school freshman Loren Shell finally walked into a therapist's office to get help. She had wanted to come for so long and at the same time didn't want to come at all. She sat down right next to her mother on the sofa in the waiting room, scanning the room for something, but she didn't know what. Noticing her mother so close, she was immediately annoyed. But she didn't move away from her.

Loren had been to a concert a month before and had felt something sharp against her skin. It was hard for her to remember now what actually happened, but she couldn't seem to shake the fear inside. She was almost sure that someone had pricked her with a needle and that she had now contracted AIDS. Even though the doctor told her this was unlikely and the test results were negative, she was still scared, almost sure she had AIDS.

"I hate it that everyone tells me that I'm okay," Loren complained. "People talk like they know. They're not in my body. And besides, I'll need another test in six months. How can they be so sure? I'm not." Loren couldn't be talked out of her irrational fears, yet her anxiety invited the people closest to her to do just that.

I've worked with adolescents for more than thirty years, both as a somatic psychotherapist and as a public school teacher. Working with teenagers can be challenging. They are, at first glance, a bundle of contradictions. Most walk in the door with two fundamental concerns. One is the need to separate from their family of origin in order to forge their own unique identity, and the other is the need to belong, have contact, and feel loved. Teenagers need to be themselves, yet they also need to know that their parents are there for them. They want to be seen, known, and appreciated, yet they are often self-conscious. In the first session with Loren I could see that she loved her mother and needed her close by, but that her mother also drove her crazy. In our initial session Loren sat very close to her mom and fought with her almost the whole time.

Loren wanted to be able to relax. She wanted some relief from the anxiety and guilt she lived inside of. "I just want to be less stressed. I spend so much of my day worrying. If it's not one thing, it's another—whether I'll do well on a test, whether I'll start in the next soccer game, whether the people that I want to hang out with want to hang out with me, or whether I'm a good or bad person." She wanted to trust the world and trust herself in the world. My first impression was that somatic work would be a good fit for her. She would learn to turn inside and meet herself. So many teenagers think the solutions to their problems lie outside themselves, and that's where they focus rather than developing the muscles of tuning into their own experience, their own sensations, toward what it is that they feel, want, and need.

So, we began with her body. I wanted Loren to become a keen somatic observer of her self. If she began to observe herself, she would gain access to the ability to shift herself. And she could gain access to this ability through somatic distinctions and practices. Being able to connect with the sensations in the body is fundamental to building somatic sensibility. If Loren could experience the sensations, she would bring more vitality and aliveness to her world and be able to relax her body, relax her whole self. Developing Loren's somatic sensibility began with an inquiry into her somatic shape.

Everyone has a unique shape. By that I mean the body is literally shaped in a particular way. Moods, emotions, thoughts, the way one coordinates with others, and the actions the adolescent takes in the world are all indicators of the somatic shape. It is critical for teenagers to be able to see and experience themselves before they can change themselves. If, for instance, they want to be close and intimate with someone but their chest collapses and their energy pulls back in their body, then their mood becomes insecure; they won't be able to be intimate. They need to look at what kind of body will produce intimacy and move toward that. Their shape determines the actions they can take in the world.

"What do you notice about your body when you study for tests?" I ask her. "I have no clue," is the first, very quick response, "except that I'm so tight that I can't stand it." "Where do you notice that tightness in your body?" This is harder for her, and I see her frustration start to rise. We go slowly here, in a mood of playing with images and feelings, almost like painting a picture of herself or building a three-dimensional model. I see that Loren's energy is high. I ask her if she can feel that. "Yeah, kind of. I know I hold my breath a lot." I notice that she holds her breath and talks through until the end of her breath. She speaks at a fast pace. At a quick glance, her body has the look of an apology, her chest slightly contracted and her eyes and eyebrows perpetually in question. I can see the tightness through her shoulders. And there is hardly any life in her lower body. This body shape is consistent with someone who lives with much anxiety.

"What do you suppose a body that was relaxed might feel like when there is an important test on the horizon?" This is too big a leap for her. "I can't even imagine," she laughs. I know that I need to teach her to slow down and experience sensation in her body. Bringing attention to the body in a mood of curiosity is foundational to somatic work. If she can connect with the lived experience of her body, she can act more powerfully in the present moment. Loren was actually interested in bringing attention inside her body to notice sensation. In fact, it was a relief for her to leave the constant rattling of her thoughts.

"Bring your attention to your feet. What do you notice about the temperature of your feet: hot, cold, cool, warm? What do you notice in terms of movement in your feet: expanding, contracting, throbbing, tingling, streaming? What do you notice are the different qualities in your feet: thick, thin, hard, soft, tight, loose? And what are the shapes or forms you might feel inside, like a burning ball of orange or a lead weight on the underside of the left foot?" Just the simple act of noticing was both soothing and interesting for her. She was authentically curious, drawn away from the normal way she looked at herself and into her own experience.

"Maybe we could do this again next time and I could lay on the sofa." She began to engage in the process from a generative place. She didn't trust the world very much, but here there was a seed of a possibility where she could relax and learn to trust herself.

Loren needed to find some place inside herself that she could trust, count on, and be connected to. In the somatic discourse she was longing for what is called a "centered presence." Being centered or embodied meant that Loren could shape herself in the world rather than being shaped by that which is outside herself. If she could learn to be centered she could be aware in the moment, present to others, and connected to her body. It didn't mean that she'd found a solution to her problems; it just meant that she had more capacity to take on what was difficult.

The process of living an embodied life is not a skill that is taught in our culture. Yet being able to drop down into yourself is something teenagers can learn. Teaching Loren how to feel her length, width, and depth, how to relax her body and her presence and move from there, allowed our therapy to reach new depths.

"Can you feel the length in your body? Can you both allow your body to be upright toward the heavens and at the same time feel yourself drop down into the earth? And can you feel your dignity and self-respect as you allow this to take shape in you?" This is one component of centering called *length*. Almost immediately she perks up. We are playing with and engaging in a new shape and she is bright enough and aware enough to smell the possibilities.

"I feel different here," she smiles slowly. "How do you feel different?" I ask. "I feel capable." With these distinctions of center, Loren begins building the capacity to tolerate uncomfortable sensations while staying balanced in the world.

I asked Loren to play with the distinctions of length, width, and depth and bring her attention to her belly. I wanted her to just notice herself in relation to these concepts. The next week she reported back about what she noticed about being centered in her soccer game. "Oh my God, I could feel myself drop when I was running. I was in me and at the same time aware of everything around me. Sometimes I could be there and sometimes I couldn't. But I know what they mean by 'the zone.' I've been there before. But this was the first time I got myself there."

This is the power of having a somatic sensibility. Somatics is pragmatic. And in the domain of being, teenagers are fiercely pragmatic. They appreciate new and effective ways of moving in the world. They are very interested in who they are, who others are, and how they can effectively belong with the people they find important. They are soaking in the very natural process of trying on new selves in the world. Working with adolescents from a somatic perspective can offer them powerful tools that are useful in building the fundamental skills of adulthood. It is scary to ask someone out on a date when you are dying to do it with every fiber of your being yet you are terrified of being rejected. Finding a pathway to the ability to be with the uncomfortable sensations that come up in your body while you are dialing the phone can be like finding gold. Almost every teenager wants to know how to feel these sensations as they arise and how to drop down into himself, his center, and let the sensations run. It is what people mean when they speak of *confidence*. One is confident when present in the body, present in the moment, filled out to the edges, connected to and able to take action toward what is of most concern. Confidence is a learnable skill.

One of the most beneficial aspects of working from a somatic perspective with adolescents is that it is fundamentally a neutral process. What happens in the body is just how it is. It can be much easier to establish trust with a teenager from this neutral place. At one point in my work with

Loren, she arrived at a session with some very specific requests. She had been chosen to work as an intern in the office of one of the elected officials in the area. Her work was primarily with adults addressing social change projects. "I'm so nervous. I want you to work with me on being able to center while I'm doing something that I don't know anything about." I smiled. To be able even to ask for that help was remarkable. In the session that day we focused on what *center* was to her, not only in her body but also in her life. "Consider that your center is what you care about." We practiced walking in the world from her belly (or what she cared about). We practiced being in conversations with people from what *she* cared about, connected to what *they* cared about. "Let yourself feel your length, width, and depth. Bring your attention to your belly and ask yourself what you care about. When you're ready, walk in the room leading from what you care about. What do you notice?" As she walked, I could see how connected to her own experience she had become. Her responses were slow and thoughtful. She could feel what she cared about. "This is great. This is great," she repeated.

At the end of the session, I asked her to continue to notice when and how she was off center. "Notice the sensations in your body of being off center. Practice ungrounding yourself and walking from that place. Allow yourself to come back to center and feel yourself walk from there. Make sure you do this in a mood of curiosity and wonder." The next time I saw her she reported that it had made a huge difference to her. She could talk to these adults, get her questions answered, and engage with them in a way that she felt good about, even when she was in an environment that she hadn't yet mastered. By observing herself and consciously practicing a new shape, some new possibility began to emerge.

One of the major differences between traditional therapy and somatic psychotherapy is the attention given to helping the client see that ultimately it is new practices that will change the self. This isn't behavior modification. This isn't just "do this" or "don't do that." Having a somatic sensibility allows an adolescent to feel how the world impacts her, and allows her to notice uncomfortable sensations and not turn away from them. In fact, it builds the capacity to drop down into the self and to consciously turn *toward* what is uncomfortable. And finally, and most importantly, somatic practices allow one to take new actions. This takes practice. As a somatic psychotherapist, I am always building the narrative around the importance of *recurrence*. Our bodies or shapes change through practice.

Somatic practices can be a lifeline for teenagers who live in challenging environments. It can be heartbreaking to watch them go back into their homes and try to survive when they can't change their circumstances. But they can learn how to pay attention to themselves and notice what they need. They can learn to become responsive to themselves. And they can build a home inside themselves, a center where they can land, feel safe, and learn to act on their own behalf. Loren, for example, has built a strong foundation of connecting with herself while connecting with the world. She has learned a place, an embodied presence, that she can purposefully access through somatic practices. She can take new actions that she was not able to take before. The seeds of self-awareness and self-trust have been planted and through practice can ripen over time.

Chapter 16

Fighting for Dignity: A Somatic
Approach to Addiction Medicine

∼ Rich Poccia

I n the last twenty or so years the treatment of addiction has transformed from smoky, back-room AA meetings into a modern science. Today, addiction medicine offers a multidisciplinary treatment for one of the most deadly problems challenging our health as a society. As we witness the continued failure of U.S. drug wars, the rise of new addiction patterns in our society, and the spread of hepatitis and HIV infections, what becomes apparent is the need to assess the problem of addiction from new perspectives.

Although my opinion is not a commonly shared one, I have long viewed addiction as an expression of a personal decision. We see in the addictive process the passion, the creative potential, and the destructive ambivalence that accompany most human endeavor. It could be argued that the potential for self-creation and self-destruction exists in conflict at the roots of this affliction. It could also be argued that all the dynamics of effort and reward are also represented here. This romantic view of addictive disease is reinforced by the fact that some of the most creative people in our society have died from or struggle with it today. Unfortunately, this tends to glorify drug use and diminish the fact that most who suffer from addictive disease die in an obscurity created by the destruction of the disease itself. For every Keith Richards there are a million unknown junkies who never get to play in the Stones. And so the questions of addictive disease remain primitive. Like any chronic and progressive disease, addiction will always address in metaphor the most complex human struggles. But the battle raging inside an addict is simpler: the successful junkie is more gratified in his efforts to become "stoned" than most people are with their efforts in the real world today. Until the addict questions the value of "stoned" at a visceral level, no change in lifestyle can take place. Why would it?

The successes of twelve-step programs indicate the importance of a spiritual recovery. Developing a spiritual center, an awareness of self—whether through traditional religion, the Salvation Army, or Alcoholics Anonymous—appears to be necessary for achieving and maintaining sobriety. For this reason, somatic therapies, specifically physical practices that increase self-awareness and develop one's relationship to one's body and the universe surrounding it, present new opportunities in the treatment of addictive disease. They both allow early intervention methods and develop lifelong tools that lead toward a balanced, centered life.

Somatics provides a path for modifying and directing oneself through the various challenges of recovery, blending it with life's natural process while diminishing the alienation commonly felt by addicts. It provides a personal freedom of choice not previously available in long-term recovery. Finally, somatics offers a method of addressing the irreversible and fatal artifacts of the disease. It helps to mediate the death experience and provides meaning and dignity, allowing for healing if not a cure.

The first somatic practices I encountered in my own recovery process were the Chinese martial arts. My decision, made early on in my sobriety, was to approach my addiction in metaphor, as a process for better understanding my experience in life. This decision provided a forward momentum that developed into an active, physical practice. Having grown up on kung fu movies and on the streets of New York City, making the move to martial arts training seemed natural. Everyone in my generation wanted to be Bruce Lee or Kwai Chang Caine. I chose to envision my life as a battle, one with a higher purpose. Since I was twenty-six years old and ridiculously self-absorbed, this approach actually worked. It provided the paradigm of the spiritual warrior not as mercenary but fighting for value and dignity in a way that held value and was a hell of a lot less embarrassing to me than "rehabilitation." The metaphor of my life's story shifted away from the stoned musician to Kwai Chang, whose natural state was "bliss." I focused on redefining "stoned," creating a new definition that allowed me to move toward a more desirable destination.

Chinese martial arts offered an acceptable and unique approach to my problem. As a somatic practice, the martial arts provided an active exploration into the disease at its physical and spiritual core. Although AA suggested that I was powerless over my addictions, these practices taught me how to look inside and simply ask why. Never in conflict with the twelve steps, the martial arts provided me a way to find out what it was that took my power or, worse, what made me give it away. To me, this seemed very reasonable. It brought back a sense of dignity I had lost. In contrast to my junkie self, my new self had to participate in my life to attain my "high." It's hard to say when the addictive process started in my life. What I can say is that I realized I had a problem falling asleep without drinking wine by the time I was eleven years old. By the age of twelve, I had added barbiturates to the mix. Ages thirteen, fourteen, and fifteen were a haze of all the above plus LSD, speed, and, finally, heroin. Once I found heroin, it became my life. From the ages of fifteen to twenty-six, my life was defined by periods of using and then not using heroin.

Life with heroin was interesting to say the least. The violence and the insanity of addiction are hard to explain. Movies like *Requiem for a Dream* and *Traffic* offer insight. Fighting and surviving take second place only to getting more drugs. The drugs are everything. The risks, the losses, and the death become so common that they eventually blur together. What you remember when it's over are the highs and the lows. In my most grandiose fantasy, I compare the experience to Ulysses having survived the songs of the Sirens. But it wasn't so noble.

My life without heroin started in 1976. The fallacy about getting sober back then was that we'd all live happily ever after. Not so. At best, you might live. But my initial commitment to developing a martial arts paradigm for my new life has proven to be the most important decision I ever made.

■ ■ ■

Living Sober

A long time ago a crusty old skid row counselor told me how he thought we, as new counselors, should approach the people entering our facility. "You remember how they used to hunt whales in the old days? You'd sneak up in a boat and stick a harpoon in 'em. Then, you just 'tie on' and expect the ride of your life. When the whale gets tired and starts circling the boat, you just reel 'em in." He said something else that rings truer today than ever before: "When they're out there [actively using], the best you can hope for is to preserve the body." In this age of HIV and the many other pathogens directly related to drug use, it is imperative to "tie on" as quickly as possible to "preserve the body."

The most difficult part of the recovery process, for both the addict and the therapist, is the beginning. Motivating the addict to develop a working relationship with the therapist and accurately assessing the problem is critical to success. As martial arts have become more mainstream in today's society, this paradigm has become more readily accepted as a somatic therapy, especially by younger addicts. A martial arts practice offers direct and nontoxic alternatives to anyone trying to address an addiction, with one major benefit: it's "très cool." Today more than ever before, everyone seems to want to be Kwai Chang again. For an addict trying to regain a place in the world, the ability to scream to the world, "I know kung fu!" like Keanu Reeves in *The Matrix* is much more appealing than saying "I'm in therapy." One represents creation and the other repair. Treating an addiction with somatics begins here. After the therapist observes the client to determine what purpose is served by the addiction, they can work together to determine the direction of treatment. A teenager using ecstasy is not telling the same story as a seasoned heroin addict. A bored housewife experimenting with marijuana is not a middle-aged cocaine addict. What story is the person telling or hiding? What does his or her body say? What is offered and what is defended? Where is the person in the process? Here, somatics offers insight and assessment that extends beyond the usual methods of traditional therapy.

I worked briefly with a Ph.D. candidate who had been drinking himself out of his program a few years before. When he stopped drinking he moved quickly toward the completion of his program and was only a few months from graduation. But now he seemed anxious and irritable all the time and was questioning his career direction. He felt he worked all the time and developed problems sleeping. He was fighting with his new girlfriend and questioned the relationship. His use of alcohol had always helped him to relax. But drinking always turned into bad mornings and missed classes. When he stopped drinking everything seemed great at first. He had more free time, his mind cleared, and he began a new relationship. But now he felt pressured in the relationship and was questioning the career decisions that he had made in the first years of his sobriety. He couldn't find the time to attend AA meetings as often as before, and he confessed that lately AA seemed simplistic. He described his sponsor, who asked him sarcastically if he thought he was now cured, as "hard core" and "tired of his bullshit." AA had become one more chore in his cluttered life.

Phineus was a first-generation Irish-American college student in his early thirties with a family history of alcoholism. Other members of his family were also in college and doing well. His parents were from the working class and were helping to pay for all the children's education, which made Phineus feel indebted. During high school Phineus had excelled in sports, but lately he felt he was getting fat because there was never time to exercise.

As we talked he paced constantly. If he settled briefly, any discussion of his problems would start him moving again, usually up and away. Frequently he turned away from me; while walking in the opposite direction he'd talk back over his shoulder. The pressure in his voice reflected his frustration at trying to explain himself.

It was obvious from the start that whatever approach we agreed on, psychology and somatics would have to blend together. Phineus had had enough education to present a well-grounded argument, but in his life he had both feet firmly planted in midair. His safety zone was secured by his accomplishments, and he wanted the story to proceed from there. His commitment to move forward in life was very much there, but the idea of being in therapy seemed like backpedaling to him. Kung fu, however, was something he'd always wanted to pursue, and he knew of its strong spiritual foundations. Since Phineus had decided to get in shape anyway, a martial arts practice "would kill two birds with one stone."

We started with a grounding and centering exercise that originated with his breath. (Not surprisingly, he perceived the importance of breathing as secondary to his form.) He held his body erect, top-heavy and forward. He generated power from his shoulders and hips while locking his breath. During stress this conditioned tendency generated more anxiety and tension, further draining his energy. Grounding opened his awareness of center and allowed him to focus on slow, even breaths. Initially, he commented on how relaxed he felt after sessions and how surprising that was considering we never actually "worked up a sweat." Breathing and refocusing produced a release of anxiety, softening and dropping his body more toward center. But as he moved into his own quiet, he seemed more reluctant to go forward. His cancellations became more frequent. Although the martial arts paradigm offered a macho enough opening for the more esoteric aspects of breath work and touch, I started to sense a lack of excitement. I had responded to his cancellations by modifying the routine so he could practice alone, keeping the responsibility of commitment on him. Maybe I was pushing too hard. Clearly, he was still circling the boat. It was time to "work up a sweat."

I added a Filipino stick-fighting technique to his solitary practice to excite his movement and further coordinate his breathing. These exercises forced concentration and focus. One can easily end up with a nasty welt if not paying attention. He enjoyed the feeling of swinging a stick and worked to develop control. With stick in hand he moved away from the esoteric, becoming more present when he practiced. He commented, "The time I practice is my own. It seems open and I enjoy the freedom of that." This opening was similar to what he experienced when he first became sober. "I just enjoy my time more. Life doesn't seem so busy." I took this as Phineus developing a sense of self away from the rat race he had been experiencing.

We started a partner exercise designed to explore distance, power, balance, and timing, all aspects of a successful martial practice. Each opened a different conversation in Phineus's body. Each offered opportunity and the chance of failure, and with each breakthrough I asked for his psychological metaphor of the experience. Distance was experienced as separation and joining. Power was speed and commitment. Balance was awareness. And we both agreed that timing is everything. By blending each aspect of his exercises until they were no longer separable, the open space he'd experienced in solitary practice was created in our relationship. In a few weeks he seemed more willing (grounded) to take risks in his life (utilizing speed, commitment, and timing) and less vulnerable to others (my attacks). In a conversation about AA he described his relationship with his sponsor as being better now. "He's all about AA and what that means to him. There are things about my life he'll never understand. But he cares about me."

A basic meditation practice provided something he and his girlfriend enjoyed together. Although I don't believe the relationship lasted, in a short time I noticed that the dramatic charge that was audible in his voice whenever he spoke about the relationship had disappeared, and the breakup was without incident.

In the period we worked together, Phineus was able to complete his program and return to the East Coast. To the best of my knowledge, he did this without drugs or alcohol. I asked his assessment of our work together. Surprisingly, he felt the most beneficial aspects of the training were the breath work and the relaxation techniques, the very things that initially bored him to tears. He moved more slowly and his voice and posture were softer. He no longer constantly paced around the room. He could talk freely, making eye contact, and not ruminate on his problems.

■ ■ ■

The Future

In America today, our lives are affected by rapid technological expansion and radical change. While some see unparalleled growth in human potential, others see an apocalyptic vision of the future. Not surprisingly, in the new search for truth and knowledge we also see an increase in drug use, ranging from the new "entheogenic" (read psychedelic) substances to heroin, speed, and all the usual suspects. The problems creating addiction have not changed. But in all the chaos, the drugs have become more sophisticated, more potent, and more available.

Somatics offers a timely and increasingly attractive method to integrate the confusion into exploration. Incorporating disciplines such as yoga, martial arts, and dance we can offer the addict an attractive support system to participate in this new world, thus eliminating the alienation common in recovery. By providing addicts with more universal interruptions of their emotions, we connect them back to their humanity and the natural developmental process that was lost in the pathology of addiction.

In AA recovery, the term "grateful alcoholic" refers to a universal concept: when the personal cost of tragedy holds value in light of the understanding gained from the experience, one becomes, in a sense, grateful for tragedy. Here is where the addict rejoins the human race. Here is where the value of being "stoned" is finally questioned. Spiritual recovery from addiction as well as most human suffering begins here.

As somatic therapists we need not reinvent the wheel but rather incorporate and integrate what is already appealing and available in our client's psyche and body. Society today seems to be asking bigger and louder versions of the same universal questions asked since the dawn of time. We need only direct them back inside.

Chapter 17

From Deadly Dance to Dance of Delight

∼ Paula Love

I had been trained to do relationship work in the usual way, having earned degrees in psychology and counseling, and I achieved a certain degree of success in helping clients move together in more delightful ways. Verbal therapy was quite useful in getting clients to recognize their recurrent patterns. But enabling them to quickly and effectively interrupt those patterns and redesign their interactions in a way that would allow them to reconnect with their passion and intimacy was another story. That process could be almost as painful as the breakdown itself!

I saw that couples would get trapped by historical conversations and ways of being that took them out of close connection with, and often estranged them from, their partners. I knew that they, like me, could often observe how their histories had created their "hot buttons." They could see how that "hot button" could be readily engaged by their partner, and that they were disempowered and ineffective at interrupting the conflict that ensued, but their clarity about this did not help them intervene in the conflicts that occurred.

I wanted to bring couples an awareness of how they move with each other, and the ability to quickly develop new ways of moving together to open deeper intimacy and greater joy. I began to refer to the painful ways partners close off intimacy as the Deadly Dance of Estrangement. Every relationship I've ever seen has one, and it often follows a well-worn path. I applied my somatic coaching training to develop a process that quickly and elegantly interrupts that dance and inspires a new one. The process can help couples effectively rechoreograph their Deadly Dance into a Dance of Delight.

■ ■ ■

Darla and Chuck
Transform Their Deadly Dance

Darla and Chuck were in the eighth year of their very committed relationship when they came to me. They were noticing a recurrent struggle between them that they had been unable to resolve on their own. There were times when each of them feared that the recurrent breakdown would cause irreparable damage to their otherwise deep connection.

Fundamentally, Darla and Chuck began their dance when Chuck would experience Darla being "snippy"; that is, lashing out at him in anger in a way that caused him to withdraw and be unavailable for interaction with her. Or the dance might start when Darla experienced Chuck as preoccupied with his own life and activities and not paying enough attention to her or to their relationship. The dance might also commence if either of them experienced some problem or breakdown at work that negatively affected their mood. For example, if Darla had had a bad day and Chuck asked her a question while she was preoccupied with what had happened at work, he might experience that his question provoked Darla's hurtful anger and hostility.

We agreed it was important to isolate and identify the basic pattern that initiated their Deadly Dance. This would provide us the opportunity to deconstruct and rechoreograph it. For Darla, it was some event that made her contract like a tight spring, that when suddenly sprung would move swiftly forward and against the person who "released" it. For Chuck, his pattern was engaged by an event that compelled him to contract and pull inward and away from the trigger, or the triggering person. In either case, once captured by their own respective patterns, Chuck and Darla were no longer present to and for each other; rather, they were in a dance with their own destructive patterning.

When we looked at Chuck and Darla's individual histories, from their early childhood to adulthood, we could see the origin of these patterns and how they were recurrently reinforced. That insight did not, however, offer them a way to intervene or interrupt the patterns.

We set about developing Darla and Chuck as astute observers of their own individual patterns. First they observed them in retrospect, with questions crafted to reveal what had happened that engaged the pattern and how it played out between them; later they observed them in real time, as the conflict was happening, developing their capacity to interrupt and intervene in it. As Darla developed a deep curiosity about her own historical pattern, she noticed the sequence of sensations in her body (tight contraction, breath high in her chest; a pause before gathering a charge, followed by heat spreading from her thighs, across her abdomen, and into her chest and face; jaw clenching), which lead to her subsequent behavior, which produced for others—especially Chuck—the feeling of being pushed away and energetically attacked.

Darla discovered how this automatic reaction was connected to her long-held expectation (of which she was largely unaware) that ultimately, in any relationship—whether family, love, or friendship—she would be abandoned or ignored or somehow pushed aside. It was as if the mechanism that constituted her ongoing experience was automatically wired to set her somatic reaction in motion whenever that mechanism (hot button) was pressed. She began to understand the anger she felt in those moments as being less about Chuck's (or anyone else's) behavior, and more as a result of her own somatic structure. That is, people would do what they did, and if they did it in a way that pressed Darla's hot button, it would set off a particular somatic sequence that produced the emotion of anger. And once angry, she would go into attack mode.

Chuck's story was similar in that he was able to connect his somatic sequence of pulling inward and away from what he interpreted as Darla's (or anyone else's) attacking behavior to his historical belief that whatever he did, it wouldn't be good enough, or wouldn't satisfy; that, unless he was perfect, he couldn't be lovable. As he began to track the sequence of his own somatic reactions when triggered, he discovered his predisposition to overreact to Darla's moods. By observing how he contracted inward, and huddled away from what felt like an attack and an accusation of unlovability, he could begin to interrupt this sequence. By allowing himself to be in a space of inquiry and a mood of curiosity, he observed that when he felt attacked or accused his chest collapsed inward, his shoulders slumped, and his head dropped slightly forward. He also began to notice that color drained from his face (he was surprised to discover that he could *feel* this happening!). His typically energetic presence would recede, and he would feel resigned. He faithfully practiced centering himself in the face of Darla's anger and finding his ground, a place to stand that allowed him to acknowledge her anger without being captured or harmed by it.

As Chuck built his capacity to tolerate Darla's anger, he also developed his capacity for compassion and understanding for what he was now beginning to think of as Darla's "vulnerability," rather than Darla's "fault." Correspondingly, Darla began to feel more accepted, and as Chuck became less triggered by her moods, she felt less scared, more assured of his love for her. This encouraged Darla to open more to Chuck, and she began to initiate more intimate conversations with him, much to his delight. Her angry outbursts decreased in frequency and intensity, and the couple moved closer to each other, having discovered their own Dance of Delight.

▓ ▓ ▓

Moving to the Dance of Delight

If you and your partner are both willing to explore your Deadly Dance, set aside some time together to do the following. Continue the exploration until you get stuck, or one or both of your moods begin to sour. When that happens, agree to stop for the time being and set another time to continue. If you continue to get stuck, you may want to consider getting support from a somatic coach who specializes in relationship issues.

With your partner:

▪ Identify the recurrent conversations between you that do not get resolved satisfactorily—where you feel stuck and angry, sad or resentful. These are the conversations where you move away from each other, engaging in avoidance or shutting down, or where you find yourselves arguing or bickering with no resolution.

▪ Identify the body sensations that occur for each of you at the very beginning of the dance.

▪ Notice what emotions occur. If you believe that there is no particular emotion, you may conclude that your emotional tendency is to "freeze" or "numb out."

▪ Identify the behavior that follows (for example, your voice gets an edge to it, you leave the room, or you engage in a verbal attack).

▪ Notice what judgments you are making about your partner (for example, "he's a jerk," "she's being unreasonable," "he's so immature," or "she's so emotional").

▪ Talk about how your sensations, emotions, behaviors, and judgments form a pattern that interferes with your producing the result you want, and how it estranges you from each other.

- Agree that whenever you find yourselves in your Deadly Dance, one of you will announce that it is occurring. Then stop the interaction to explore your respective body sensations, emotions, behaviors, and judgments. Repeat this process as many times as necessary until both of you are so aware of the process that you can interrupt the Deadly Dance earlier and earlier. If this is too difficult to do on your own, consider consulting a Somatic Coach.

- Learn practices such as centering and grounding, and turning toward the "grab." (A coach can teach them to you.) Practice them and use them.

Remember that this process is not easy, but with the support of a coach—and your serious commitment to observing and practicing—you can interrupt the dance and design new steps, performing the Dance of Delight more often, and more consistently.

Chapter 18

From Surviving to Thriving

~ Jennifer Cohen

Most of all I wanted to understand. I wanted to understand the terror in my body, the sensation of having weight on me when no one was there, the unexplained movements of my body in the night, the fear I felt when someone—even someone I loved—approached from the "wrong" angle. I wanted to understand the images of horror that came to me in the most inappropriate of moments. I wanted to understand why I felt like I was dying most of the time. So often my body was giving me signals that I did not know how to interpret: chronic pain, urinary tract infections, feelings of anxiety and emptiness, rage that felt like it was eating away at my capacity to love anyone or anything.

Not until I began to look at my pain through the lenses of trauma and somatics did I begin to feel something new emerge. Some sense of my sanity began to appear—some deep sense of hope for my life—and a new and rich context in which to unwind and rebuild myself from the ground, upward and outward back into the world, began to make itself known.

To this day people come to me after years of traditional psychotherapy. Grateful as they are for the work done there, they often say, "Something is missing." Insight coupled with some strategies for building a new way of being for their life does not allow them to complete the history of trauma, nor does it allow them to enter a new and powerful phase of self-actualization. It does not allow them to feel safe in the world, nor are they competent to be at the center of their own life and to design their future free

191

from the constraints of the terror that gripped their physiology when they were being abused. A woman came to me after ten years of psychotherapy related to her history of child sexual abuse. In all that time she had not been able to complete a visit to her gynecologist. After nine months of working with me she was able, among other things, to complete a gynecological exam for the first time.

Trauma places numerous constraints on a person's capacity to live powerfully in the world. It is true in my experience, both personal and professional, that trauma carves pathways in the body and mind so deep they may not be erased in this life. It is equally true that a person can carve new pathways. Trauma is a powerful teacher. It teaches people to survive anything. It acquaints people with fear and terror. It teaches us to take nothing for granted: not safety, not love, not our own bodies as home, nothing. It teaches people to live constantly on alert, waiting and ready for the next thing to happen. Trauma forces people to question the nature of good and evil, and it leaves people feeling that there is something terribly wrong with them. The ways people learned to survive the events of their past often make it impossible to design a life free of fear.

■ ■ ■

Stephanie

Stephanie came to me after years of psychotherapy. She was small in stature, with an obvious edge of anger in her voice. She would say something and then let out a slight chuckle, as if she were uncomfortable having spoken. Her pelvis was retracted and she always pulled her feet off the ground when sitting across from me. Her body would end up in a curved shape, like a bow. She made herself smaller and smaller as she spoke. She stated that she often felt overpowered by other people and took care of them at the expense of her own well-being. Stephanie struggled with depression and several failed relationships over the years.

As we began to work somatically, Stephanie would experience waves of terror. Her body would recoil, she would cry, and then she would actually freeze up, her breathing high and slight, eyes frozen, skin pale, voice all but inaudible, her life force visibly squelched, unable to make any contact with me. She looked just like that abused child. She reported feeling gone, like she had left her body. The fear in the room was palpable. She *was* gone. It was as if I were touching an empty shell of a human being.

Her body knew this pathway well. She had felt terror most of her life. She told me she never felt safe and felt that she "might as well not bother to exist" she was so unimportant. Self-hatred permeated her everyday life. She pulled herself "up and out" of her own body and stopped the overwhelming flood of sensation and emotion that was occurring.

The abuse Stephanie experienced, which by definition happened against her will, and against her sense of herself as a human being with power and rights, called into question her right to exist in her body on this earth. Every time she felt frightened she would recreate the patterned response of leaving. She did not even know she had a right to exist.

■ ■ ■

The anthropologist and author Angeles Arian wrote that "Belonging is the other side of Longing." The longing to belong is part of our primate legacy. We are descended from creatures that thrive in communities. Someone in Stephanie's family abused her, and others did not keep her safe from that abuse. Although her biological legacy compels her to move toward connecting with others, her personal history compels her to avoid connecting deeply. Stephanie longs for contact and connection yet recoils in fear of another betrayal. Whom can she trust? In what can she believe? Being present was too intolerable, so she left. Every time she attempts to return to herself, she is flooded with sensations and patterns of being that catapult her out again. She says she has no sense of where she belongs, "not a leg to stand on." When Stephanie sits in her chair and tucks her legs up underneath her, that belief is strikingly visible.

With these beliefs firmly embodied, Stephanie is never at rest. Abuse creates a kind of vigilance in a person, making her always alert, always on guard, never able to relax inside her own skin, unable to trust that the ground underneath will catch her, unable to know she is home somewhere, anywhere. This is an exhausting way to be. Stephanie is almost always tired and often does not sleep well; the strain eats away at her mood, her hope, her health, and her well-being. By the time she was thirty, Stephanie had her first experience with cancer.

■ ■ ■

The Ecology of Healing

This is the temple
of my adult aloneness
And I belong
To that aloneness
As I belong to my life.

There is no house
Like the house of belonging.

—*David Whyte,* "The House of Belonging"

How do we find our way home from such a terrible violation? I contend that the work of restoration calls us back to the scene of the original horror, the body, asks us for the truth, and then requires reconciliation.

Somatics teaches that the body is our access to the earth. Our feet touch the ground and make contact. We walk firmly or tentatively, with authority or as if we are asking permission to take the next step. Stephanie, not believing that her thoughts, feelings, and opinions mattered, could not find her ground. She was often like a leaf blowing in the wind, not able to stand for anything, unable to take her authority back, until at last I was able to show her how to put her feet on the ground through somatic practice. This connection with oneself through ground alone, although not exclusively, distinguishes the work of somatic coaching from other disciplines dedicated to helping survivors of violence recover. Never before had Stephanie been offered a method for actually being competent to take back the authority she was trained to relinquish through the violence she experienced.

Re-entering the body was a terrifying experience for Stephanie. At first the sensations reminded her of the original abuse. This provided a good moment to begin to re-educate and update the nervous system. Trapped in a pattern of flight and freeze, her body was still replaying the abuse scene. Stephanie would literally feel as if the abuse were still happening. She reported feeling "unsafe" when she began to feel sensations in her body. Stephanie reported believing that if she began to feel what she had been dissociating from, she would drown in an unending flood of grief and pain and would not recover.

Experiencing the terror in the present is an opportunity to release what is backlogged in a methodical and controlled context. Stephanie learned to observe what arose and ground the sensations through contact, observation, breath, and pacing. Pema Chodron, a beloved Buddhist monk and teacher, states that, "A mystic is swimming in the same water a psychotic is drowning in." Stephanie needed to learn how to swim in her own sensations. With practice she became more familiar with the process of noticing her breath and identifying sensations without moving into a story about her history. She began to find out what was most basic to her: her own life force, her own breath, her own rhythm. Stephanie was beginning to find the ground on which to stand.

Some say that the breath is the physical link between the body, the mind, and the spirit. Coming from the word "*re*spiration," connected to the word "*in*spiration," to breathe means, among other things, to bring in one's spirit to the body. When someone experiences fear, one of the first things they do is hold their breath. Some people, after the original trauma, never settle down enough to let their breath back out. At the beginning of our work, Stephanie's breath was often high and quite shallow.

Try it. Take a moment and hold your breath. Watch as your lungs fill, your chest expands, and your muscles tighten. Imagine never letting that go. Always holding on tightly, waiting, watching.

It is amazing to watch what happens when I ask people to breathe deeply. In the beginning, when I asked Stephanie to breathe deeply, she would almost instantly move into a state of fear. With time, however, something interesting started to happen. She began to deeply relax for the first time. Breathing deeply in new patterns began to carve new pathways in her being. Her body lengthened. The crust of anger softened into the well of grief beneath and she began to be able to tolerate her own sensations, the sensations and pulsations that make up the very foundation of her existence. And they were her sensations, belonging only and wholly to her. No one could take them away; no one could say they were not real. This was fundamental and life altering.

In my work with survivors of trauma, I would ask clients to report on their sensations and what they were experiencing in their bodies at any given moment. Within moments many clients would be reporting on sensations in others people's bodies. They would dissociate into memories of other people and begin to talk about the other person's feeling states and experiences, unable to stay connected to their own. They literally could not stay in their own bodies long enough to know what was happening or what they were experiencing for themselves. They could, however, detail what was going on for lots of other people, at times with remarkable accuracy. In many ways this skill, and it is a skill, had served these clients. They were deeply empathic toward others and could read people, something that benefited them a great deal in their lives. However, they could not easily stand up for themselves. Not knowing where their own boundaries were was costing them dearly.

With time, attention, and patience, it is possible for survivors of trauma to find their way back to their own sensations, to find out what they are thinking and feeling, and where their boundaries are. Their relationship to themselves and to others can change. With the touch of my hand and the contact between us, clients could begin to feel where they began and ended and where I began and ended. By developing their capacity to stay present with their own sensations and feelings, they could find their own edges and not keep their total attention on the next potential attack. Knowing where they were and what they would and would not tolerate gave them a whole new sense of power in the world. They had returned to themselves as the center of their own existence, and with that power came a whole new way of being in the world.

Because of sexual abuse, my clients did not know how to stay connected to their own experience while extending themselves toward another. I asked them to stand facing me, our bodies three feet apart. Now that they had become skillful at noting their own sensations, I asked them to include making eye contact with me as they stayed connected to their own emotions and sensations and to the experience of having their feet firmly planted on the ground. At first this was nearly impossible. With practice, however, they were able to stay inside of their own body boundaries and extend their life energy, attention, and love toward me and then toward others in their lives.

When I first suggested that Stephanie use her voice in the work, she could barely make a sound. I would invite her to make a sigh or a sound as she exhaled and she would once again begin to shrink and curl up, her body still playing out the pattern of disappearance and resignation. Slowly her voice got louder and stronger, and as it did, so did she. She moved from resignation about her voice never being heard again to rage that her voice had been disregarded in the first place. She began to respect herself and her own wants and needs and began to learn how to ask for what she needed and wanted in a relationship. These new-found competencies changed the way she related to her lover, her friends, and herself.

I might ask my clients that they make sounds in between sessions, on a daily basis, and that they begin a practice of speaking when they feel themselves beginning to "disappear." With time and practice they are able to sustain sound and begin to speak in situations where they would have previously been silent. They begin to reassert their humanity where they would have previously been invisible. This new skill impacts their whole way of being in the world. At the end of one year most can stay with their own experiences. They can successfully express their needs and wants and move powerfully in their personal and professional lives.

The experience of finding your own sensations, feeling the ground underneath you as yours, feeling your own boundaries and learning to respect them, and finally hearing the power of your own voice honored and respected is an experience powerful enough to carve new pathways in body and mind. These are pathways that a person can find again and again, allowing him or her to take powerful new action and invent a future not defined by the legacy of trauma.

As people become capable of observing themselves from moment to moment, and as they develop the capacity to articulate what is arising in the body and the mind, as they become able to shift from a historical pattern to a new way of being present moment to moment, something wonderful happens. People begin to tap into a kind of wisdom that comes from deep contact with a truth that arises only when one is truly available to hear it and know it. It is the truth of the moment; paying attention to what is so and being able to bring our full attention to it.

The work of somatic coaching offers a powerful framework for transformation. In order to live beyond the constraints of a history of trauma, one must: take back one's power, build a capacity to stand for oneself powerfully and skillfully, take action on one's own behalf, fight for one's dignity and respect, and extend into the world while remaining fully present to one's own experience of life in the moment. This set of tools offers people not only deep understanding of the impact of history, it offers a way of living in the world that allows people to complete what is incomplete and move into the future with grace and fluidity.

Chapter 19

The Power of Somatics in Sobriety

∼ J. Clare Bowen-Davies

Choice follows awareness.

—*Richard Strozzi-Heckler*

A decade ago, at a dual-diagnosis chemical dependency treatment center in Orange County, California, we attempted to motivate our clients by saying that only one in thirty would actually stay clean and sober following discharge. Although today I am embarrassed by that approach and wonder what were we thinking, I must also acknowledge that the number of alcoholics and addicts staying in long-term recovery is in fact discouraging. The statistics are limited by the anonymous nature of the one organization involved worldwide in recovery, but we have come to accept in the recovery field that many do not stay clean and sober. With the treatment knowledge I have today, this is of great concern and simply unacceptable.

Traditional addiction treatment involves mostly intellectual endeavors: cognitive belief shifting, gaining insight, conscious choice, and group process. On the action front there is time structuring and behavior change. Twelve-step programs, such as Alcoholics Anonymous, Narcotics Anonymous, Codependents Anonymous, and Overeaters Anonymous, are also utilized. Engaging in a twelve-step program includes attending meetings regularly (ninety meetings in the first ninety days is common, then two to three times per week thereafter), actually working through the twelve steps with a sponsor (otherwise known as a mentor), and taking "one day at a time." Although some inpatient treatment facilities pay attention to the body and its sensations, they are in the minority.

Having worked with hundreds of clients over the years, I am convinced there is one approach that could be easily integrated into treatment programs and counseling offices that would make an enormous difference. This is the approach of somatics, which embraces the potent existence of the body. Staci Haines writes in *The Survivor's Guide to Sex*, "Somatics recognizes an intelligence and life in the body that affects your thinking and your actions. If you change your body ... then your thinking, your experience of the world, and often your identity will also shift." It is my commitment to bring somatics to the recovering community.

My commitment here is a reflection of being at one with this work. I "get" the internal black hole that alcoholics and addicts have because I have it too. I've been sober now fourteen years and state with certainty that managing my black hole is an easy task these days, based more on the somatic work I've done than the duration of my sobriety. Inviting myself back into my body, which I vacated years ago, has been a truly awesome experience, ranging from sheer terror at one end of the scale to unbelievable joy at the other.

■ ■ ■

Working with Addiction

I choose to specialize in working with addiction in spite of the work's immense frustrations. It's frustrating because addicts and alcoholics fail so often. You'd think it would be easy to just walk past the bar, drive past the liquor store, or avoid the dealer's house. "Just say no!" How hard could that be?

"Just say no" is one of the most ineffective pieces of advice ever given. The body does not recognize such an intellectual directive. Take, for example, Beth, twenty-nine, a cocaine addict who knows intellectually that snorting that line of coke is harmful, risky, costly, and actually downright stupid, and yet she does it anyway. Her intellectual knowledge is not enough to interfere with the power of the body. The body has become compelled and habituated to take the action involved; the habit has actually become *embodied*. Beth reports that she doesn't remember what happens between seeing her drug of choice and being under the influence; she is simply on automatic pilot.

Then there's Jim. Jim is a super-smart engineer, owns a business, and is fundamentally a man with demons. He's a Vietnam vet who's been medicating his appalling memories with alcohol for decades. Why should he face his night terrors when he can drift into oblivion with the help of a pint of vodka? Jim reports there have been times when he has a vague recollection of being on his way to the grocery store, and the next thing he remembers is waking up in a dark hotel room several days later, with a horrific hangover and a desire to just end the pain. He too is on automatic pilot. On seeing the alcohol in the store, his body's desires are stronger than his intellectual knowledge that alcohol is destroying his life.

At its core, addiction encompasses a habitual set of routines and rituals, otherwise known as practices, repeated over time. Anything we do repetitively over time we get good at: this is both the good news and the bad news. *We are our practices.* We embody what we practice. Consider how when we drive it's as if we're on automatic pilot. We don't have to concentrate on unlocking the door, putting the key in the ignition, putting on our seatbelt, engaging a gear, letting off the brake, and steering down the street; it's embodied.

■ ■ ■

Embodiment

An excellent example of embodiment is Tiger Woods. Although he is gifted, this is a man who has practiced the art of golf on a daily basis since he could walk. Through recurrence and repetition he has imprinted his body with the ability to swing a golf club, assess distance and spin, compensate for wind and a sloping green, and accurately target the hole. Does he have to stop and consciously think about what to do, where to place his hands on the club, how far apart his feet should be? No, these are automatic, natural, unconscious actions, embedded as muscle memory—embodied. Instead he's paying attention to his mood and attitude, creating the will and desire to win.

Something we all embody is the ability to cross our arms: go ahead and do this now. You'll notice one hand is tucked, one hand is revealed. Now fold your arms the other way. Weird, isn't it? Most of us have difficulty here, because we have to stop and think about an action that is opposite to our natural tendency. I use this exercise to illustrate the process of change. Most people come to coaching or counseling with a desire to change some habitual behavior or belief, and we experiment with how this process is going to feel—clunky, weird, and awkward, with a pull to return to the natural tendency we already have. So change may be simple, but it's not easy.

If addiction is fundamentally a habitual set of self-destructive routines and rituals, then they must be replaced with new routines and rituals supporting abstinence from mood- and mind-altering substances. Anne Fletcher's book *Sober for Good* is an exploration of the techniques that "masters" of recovery have used to maintain sobriety without traditional twelve-step programs. One of the masters, Charles, speaks of "finding time to calm and center [yourself], while in the past, alcohol was the ritual that allowed the centering." He has established a series of new rituals to replace the tradition of drinking and all that lead there. Starting the day with a clear head allows him to meditate, contemplate affirmations, lift weights, run, and eat a good breakfast, creating the possibility for a satisfying, sober day ahead.

■ ■ ■

Addicts and Their Practices:
Preparation Rituals

Diane, a street-wise long-term heroin addict, is now determined to get clean for the sake of the child she carries in her womb. Since she began injecting heroin intravenously, she's been engaged in a complex ritual to prepare and administer her drug of choice. The ritual and administration is completely embodied. It involves a spoon, needle, cotton, flame, tourniquet, and white powder, all woven together in an elaborate series of predictable actions.

Anthony has been rolling marijuana joints since puberty. Mandy enjoys squeezing the slice of lime into her bottle of Tecate and has done so for as long as she can remember. Roger is compelled to purchase a particular kind of cigarette lighter for his dope. Katie finds pleasure in taking out a new razor blade, watching its edge shine in the candlelight, cutting the coke on the mirror, rolling up a "lucky" $100 bill to snort, and plunging into joyous oblivion.

The extent and importance of these preparation rituals cannot be underestimated. They are all as embodied as your action in squeezing the toothpaste out of the tube onto the toothbrush, and where you begin to brush your teeth. Extinguishing these rituals and replacing them with sobriety-oriented rituals takes commitment on the part of the client, and skill on the part of the practitioner.

■ ■ ■

Somatic Practices for Recovery

I teach clients how to become present in their bodies, how to identify sensations, and how to become aware of what's going on other than their thoughts. Naturally, in order to teach these practices I have to be present in my own body: present, open, and connected, fully available to my clients and their process. I check in with myself. Am I grounded? Am I breathing deeply and rhythmically? Am I letting go of invasive thoughts? Am I fully in the moment? To ensure I am all these things I've designed my own private routines involving paying attention to the breath, meditation, yoga, exercise, dance, affirming mantras, and so on. I also get regular bodywork.

When I work with clients we begin by paying attention to the breath. Most people breathe with an incredible shallowness, the top part of the chest, below the throat, rising and falling slightly, the remainder of the chest cavity remaining still. The rib cage is designed to expand and contract as the lungs fill with air, the diaphragm (attached around the base of the rib cage) to move up and down, extending movement into the belly. Singers are trained in diaphragmatic breathing, so that if they put their hands on the sides of their ribcage just above the waist, there is perceptible movement outwards. Experiment with that for yourself now.

The next stage is to become grounded and centered. Coming from the martial arts tradition, grounding and centering are the processes by which we become present in the body. They are the antithesis of "being out to lunch," "off center," "ungrounded," "a space case." Breathing deeply, we drop our attention to the belly. Eastern traditions point to the *hara* or *tantiens*, two inches below the belly button, as the physical and energetic center of the body. When attention is dropped into the belly (which is different than thinking about the belly), it is possible to experience the full power of being present in the body, allowing the body to be a domain of action, not just the physical structure we have as humans. It's not what you *know* but what you can *do*, what *action* you can be in. It's about having bodily awareness in the center of the abdomen rather than the head or shoulders, which is where most of the Western world lives. When movement is initiated from this potent energetic center (rather than leading with the head), we are more present, powerful, compelling, and successful.

Let's return for a moment to an earlier premise, that alcoholics and addicts spend much of their life on automatic pilot. The natural antidote to automatic pilot is to be present in the body, and the process of centering described above is the way to become present. This is the fundamental reason it is critical for those in recovery to reverse the trend their body has followed for decades. Becoming present to the triggers of the environment, feelings, moods, and emotions, alcoholics/addicts in recovery now have a choice about what they do. Their automatic pilot organized around their drug of choice is replaced with an automatic pilot organized around activities that maintain their sobriety. Consequently, they can achieve significant improvement in the quality not just of their sobriety, but of their lives as a whole.

■ ■ ■

Kevin: Successful in Sobriety

Kevin has made outstanding progress in quitting a thirty-year marijuana addiction. What's of particular interest is that Kevin came to treatment with an already-developed ability to pay attention to the breath and to ground and center due to a five-year martial arts practice. This is quite unusual and I believe has made a dramatic contribution to Kevin's ability to get and stay clean and sober.

Kevin is a slender, anxious, long-haired man just turned forty, who has drifted from job to job since his brief experience in the Army in his late teens (the choice at the time was jail or the military due to drug charges). He has been smoking marijuana daily since the age of ten, and he has also used cocaine, speed, mushrooms, LSD, and alcohol. His use escalated in the military, and he received a dishonorable discharge. He later married but was divorced after only a couple of years. He acknowledges another powerful addiction—his sexual addiction—contributed to the end of the marriage.

Divorce elicited a suicide attempt, and during a brief hospitalization professionals began to confront him about his marijuana dependence. This proved to be the beginning of the classic "hitting bottom" experience and led to his seeking out professional help.

Most addicts come to treatment with little or no structure in their lives, and the first task was to design his time away from work. With an hourly chart in hand, he left the first session to fill his time with healthy activities, including expanding his martial arts practice and spending more time with his horse.

Another valuable and effective intervention for Kevin is what I call "body-oriented thought stopping." As soon as he's aware of having been triggered by something, either internally or in the environment, and begins to have euphoric recall about smoking marijuana, he takes a deep breath, visualizes a traffic stop sign or a red stoplight, takes another deep breath, grounds and centers, and then immediately changes his activity. Stopping the thought and staying still has little to no effect. *Movement* is a critical component: he must brush his teeth, go for a walk, get a drink of water, take a shower, or talk to a friend. The body-oriented thought stopping technique utilizing attention to the breath has been remarkably powerful, and he's now transferring this skill to manage his sexual fantasies about women, with positive results.

Kevin and I both believe his notable progress in sobriety is a reflection of his already-embodied skills in paying attention to the breath and grounding and centering, courtesy of his martial arts practice. It's like having a box of matches when everyone else has two twigs to rub together. I have worked with no other client with such a history who was able to smoke for the last time after our first appointment and stay clean and sober from then on. Kevin has abstained from marijuana (and all other substances, including alcohol) for nearly nine months at the time of writing this, and he is beginning to set goals for the future. He's clearing up "the wreckage of his past": getting his finances in order so he can buy a home, taking classes to expand his career opportunities, making contact with his birth and adoptive families, and grieving the loss of his marriage.

■ ■ ■

Sandy: A Focus on Survival

Sandy, the twenty-five-year-old daughter of prosperous parents, turned her back on an opulent lifestyle when she was introduced to cocaine by a boyfriend and rapidly became addicted. Less than a year after discovering cocaine she had been kicked out of her apartment and was living in her car with a dog named Boxer, pretty much her only friend now. She stayed in motels when she could afford to; it was just plain easier to get loaded there, in private. She developed a strategy for raising money for her drugs and accommodation. Wearing one of her old, expensive outfits, kept in good shape, she would go to a luxury store and shoplift clothes, then return them with a sob story about a lost receipt.

I was always sad to hear the story of how she woke up each morning, her first concerns being: Will I get arrested today? Where will I shoplift today? Will I have to sleep with someone for coke or speed? Which connection will come through with product? Will I be able to get a room tonight, or will I sleep in the car?

Addiction creates an obsession, repetitive, compulsive behavior and complete preoccupation with the drug of choice. It's no surprise to learn that alcoholics and addicts struggle to have intimate relationships with people: their lives are organized, by definition, around their drug of choice. Their drug is predictable, reliable, effective, and joy- and oblivion-inducing. Mere people don't stand a chance.

Sandy and I began our work together after she had completed a thirty-day residential treatment program. She was fortunate enough to have a family still willing to offer financial support. She had previously completed a model mugging course, and I immediately referred her to a second one. Having previously participated in this adrenaline-state training, she had some notion of embodiment and could immediately use somatically enhanced thought-stopping techniques.

In addition, I suggested she adopt a yoga practice to promote awareness of breathing and presence in the body. Being present in this way initially induced fear in her (due to past trauma and consequent dissociation). Over time she transformed not only the way in which she was able to relate to her body, but also the way she handled opportunities for relapse. Faced many times with the opportunity to use cocaine or speed since her recovery began, she reports that she now has the ability to get present in her body by paying attention to her breathing, getting centered, and from this place of awareness making the choice to stay clean. This is an incredible ability for Sandy to have developed, coming to treatment as she did, without friends and living in her car. She had no choice then. She's now created multiple choices in her life. She's empowered and living a full life.

■ ■ ■

Conclusion

I've related stories about the successes in applying the somatic approach to recovery, not the failures. For every client successful in maintaining recovery, there are a dozen who are not. It's not about financial resources, or going to enough twelve-step meetings, or having a spiritual connection, or really, really wanting to be sober (although these things help). It's about realizing you have a body and that there's value to experiencing the sensations of the body. It's about befriending it and courageously exploring being present in the body and all that means, especially to alcoholics and addicts. It's about living with joy and gratitude in the body.

What is the next level of development for the addictions recovery field? As Christine Caldwell has said in *Getting Our Bodies Back: Recovery, Healing and Transformation through Body-Centered Psychotherapy* "I believe it lies in the area of recovering our bodies, and working with addiction's deepest root: physical desensitization and habituation." With the kind of information we have today about the crucial role of somatics in addiction and recovery, it is no longer acceptable for us to tolerate a low level of success in treatment. Personally, I will be satisfied only when somatic practices are incorporated in the mainstream of addiction treatment. I wish for all recovering people the possibility of an empowered, embodied, bold sober life.

Chapter 20

Conquering Chronic Headaches: Somatic Self-Care for Transforming Pain

~ Jan Mundo

C harles used to visit my office in the throes of a three-day sick migraine. He began each visit nauseated and so weak that he could barely hold his head up; his face emitted a gray-green pallor. Forty years old, he had been dealing with his migraines, using one medication or another, since he was twelve. Following my one-hour headache treatment, his color would turn from green to white, and his posture would straighten. He would announce that his headache was gone and that he was hungry and ready to go home, eat, and sleep.

Charles is one of an estimated forty to fifty million people in the United States who experience chronic headaches. Fifteen to twenty-five million of them are debilitated by migraines, two-thirds of whom are women. Research studies show that employers and workers spend an astonishing $1.3 billion each year on medical treatment for chronic headaches. Missed and inefficient work due to headaches and migraines takes an even greater toll on businesses with an additional $13 billion in lost productivity annually.[1]

These statistics provide ample evidence that the conventional approach to prevention and treatment of chronic headaches doesn't work. I invite you to explore a new approach, *somatic self-care*, which provides people with real solutions for ending the cycle of chronic pain.

■ ■ ■

The Conventional Approach

Marla had a fourteen-year history of daily "mixed" headaches, a combination featuring the worst symptoms of both tension and migraine headaches. The headaches were pulsing, pounding, and nauseating. She had been taking Excedrin, an over-the-counter pain preparation meant for short-term use, nearly every day for fourteen years. Marla enrolled in and completed one of my programs sponsored by the health education department of a health maintenance organization. Despite my assessment that she was habituated to her remedy and that it was causing rebound headaches, Marla insisted that her pills were the only thing keeping her from even more severe pain.

Many people who suffer from chronic headaches are like Marla. All they care about is staying still and doing whatever they can to stop their pain and related symptoms. They take one prescribed medication for relief, another for prevention, an antidepressant, plus an over-the-counter pain or sinus preparation. If those don't work, they may even go to the emergency room for a shot of Demerol.

Unfortunately, the pharmacologic approach to headaches is not without serious side effects. These vary according to precise medication taken but often include dizziness, loss of appetite, nausea, vomiting, diarrhea or constipation, gastric bleeding, and sedation, not to mention an increased risk of stroke. The most troubling consequence of regular intake (more than fifteen times per month) is medication overuse, which causes the patient to suffer rebound headaches, sometimes daily, as soon as the level of medication in the bloodstream is reduced. Thus, patients have a strong incentive—increased episodes of pain—to continue their chronic reliance on drug therapy. In a study presented at the 2001 International Headache Congress, the triptans, formerly an invincible family of headache drugs, were shown to be the most quickly habituating when compared to opioids and analgesics. Medication overuse can be caused by frequently combining analgesics, opioids, ergot alkaloids, and triptans.[2]

■ ■ ■

My Path to Headache Healing

My own lack of success with over-the-counter headache medications prompted me to find a new approach for my premenstrual migraines. In 1970, my lifestyle was changing: I was spending more time in nature, I became a vegetarian and a meditator, and accordingly sought more natural remedies. I learned about a claim that one could stop headaches simply by placing the hands on the head. I tried doing so and found that indeed I could stop a headache cold in minutes, both for myself and others. Strange as it sounds, I could feel the headache and move it out.

From then on I became a magnet for people who had headaches. Everywhere I went—a business, social, or family event, or even shopping—someone would exclaim, "Oh God! I've got such a headache." Delighted to help, but without thinking much about what I was actually doing, I would offer to relieve their pain. After about five minutes of my specialized hands-on therapy, my surprised and delighted subjects would thank me and resume their normal activities, now pain free.

If I was to be successful, I realized, I would need to do two things: become a conscious observer of my method, and learn more about headaches. I began by transcribing my experience from touch to written word and discovered that I had been working with the same cycle of sensations each time—that is, all headaches had a predictable course that could be felt, altered, and released, and at each stage there were subtle, identifiable cues that, when complete, signaled relief for the client. I translated this protocol into written instructions for self-application and tested them on people with a history of migraine to see if the instructions worked. I found that my informal test subjects were indeed able to relieve their headaches independently.

So now I knew that my method worked, but I still knew little about the symptomatology and known causes of headaches. I began researching the consumer and medical literature and was surprised and disappointed to find out that, despite billions of dollars spent on research, the exact mechanism of headaches is unknown. This was provocative: I wondered if understanding more about my hands-on therapy might provide a key to discovering a piece of the headache puzzle.

In reading, I learned that current medical treatment for headaches is often costly, lengthy, and frustrating for patients and practitioners alike. Despite the best modern therapies, chronic headache problems can persist for years, even decades, while their underlying causes remain unaddressed. Patients feel increasingly hopeless, helpless, and overwhelmed. In their attempts to be free of pain and other symptoms, they try a bevy of medications from a variety of practitioners. They feel that no one is listening anymore, and although at first they fight their doctors' words, "You just have to live with it," eventually they learn to accept them.

My learning didn't stop with reading. I trained in a variety of modalities, including massage therapy, energy work, intuitive development, and body-centered therapies, including breathwork, chi gung and mindfulness meditation, Core Shamanism, Somatic Coaching™, and Somatic Bodywork™.

▪ ▪ ▪

A Self-Care Program Produces Results

Combining my training and a review of the headache literature, including Dr. Rodolfo Low's research on diet and migraines,[3] I designed a self-care relief and prevention program that teaches people how to naturally find and eliminate the underlying causes of their headaches and migraines, along with methods to alleviate their pain and related symptoms. I have taught the Mundo Program through health education courses at health maintenance organizations, medical centers, universities, and corporations for the last ten years.

A preliminary retrospective study conducted in October 2000 and later published in abstract form in the International Headache Journal, *Cephalalgia* (May 2001), demonstrated the Mundo Program's benefits to patients and its potential cost-effectiveness for healthcare organizations.[4] The study describes seventy-eight migraine patients who completed my six-week program, which included identification and elimination of headache triggers, body-centered awareness, breathing, and therapeutic hands-on techniques. The participants had a median of nineteen headache years, which means that some people had them for a year, and some for forty years! Researchers found a forty-one percent reduction in the number of headaches, a fifty-two percent reduction in abortive medications, with ninety-seven percent reporting that they felt more in control and had greater understanding of their headache pattern.

This model, with its untapped ability to reduce lost labor costs due to migraine, has promising implications for the workplace. If workers could benefit from the Mundo Program with the same forty-one percent reduction in their headaches that the study participants had, then employers could save an estimated $5.3 billion of the $13 billion that they lose annually due to decreased productivity from migraine.

■ ■ ■

An Alternative to Conventional Therapies: The Somatic Approach

My approach is a somatic approach, and as such it involves awareness of the whole self—body, mind, spirit, and emotions. Somatics, derived from the Greek for "living body," defines the body as a dynamic, functional expression of the self rather than a collection of mechanical parts. In Western societies, we seem to live mostly in our heads, with the attitude that the body is only a convenient vehicle on which to carry the head. Many people become aware of their body only during exercise or physical activity. Worse, people who suffer chronic pain ignore and withdraw their attention from their body for so long that they only begin to feel their body at the point of pain. In contrast, somatics teaches that the body is a reflection of who we are and the life we are living—it is our base of support. By recognizing it as such, people can discover effective ways to work with their chronic pain.

But how can somatic awareness heal headaches when the best of modern medicines cannot? A somatic self-care program addresses an entirely different realm from that addressed by standard medical treatment—and even some alternative therapies. In somatics, the treatment is the process. A pill doesn't address how you collect stress in your shoulders or clench your jaw. A pill can't identify when your breathing is shallow and held. Neither does it teach you how these factors can contribute to your headaches, nor how to change them to produce a better outcome. It seems simple, but by learning how to pay close attention to yourself and your daily actions, and then modifying or substituting other actions, you can actually solve your personal migraine mystery once and for all.

■ ■ ■

Somatics As a Means of Taking Control

Somatics works because it empowers individuals to take control of their healing. In a recent survey, migraine patients said they wanted to be more in control of their own care and learn ways to relieve and prevent their headaches.[5] This is also exemplified in a classic workplace stress study, in which people who identified the cause of their problem as being outside themselves felt that they had no control over it, with slim chance of changing their behavior.[6]

Whereas conventional headache treatment puts the situation in the hands of physicians and drugs, a somatic approach empowers the headache patient to take personal responsibility for their pain and their care. Allopathic medicine encourages patients to look for solutions outside themselves, to take drugs to stop their pain in the moment, and not to ask themselves how they may have gotten it in the first place. Over time, their pain becomes so mixed in with the fear of its imminence and the memories of past pain episodes that their reaction becomes part of the problem and they feel even more out of control. The somatic approach doesn't involve "blaming the victim" for their illness, but rather asks that they step outside the box to carefully examine themselves. Looking within produces awareness. This in turn gives people more options for responding and, in the long run, more control over their thoughts and actions.

Restated in the positive, people who identify with their ability to control their problem internally can produce change. I found it very interesting that in the Mundo Program study cited above, although researchers found a forty-one percent reduction in migraines, ninety-seven reported they felt better. In the survey comments, they described changes they made and the resultant improvements in the quality of their work and personal lives. They knew more about their headaches and their options for responding, and thus felt more in control.

Sonya, a woman in her late thirties who was referred to my class by a neurologist, would consistently enter the classroom in a sullen mood, with her head down. Her skin had a gray tinge. She was thin, wan, drank lots of coffee, had a stressful job, was constantly worried, and never exercised. The intensity of her migraines was fed by her fear of having a brain tumor, though all tests were negative. Two weeks into the six-week course, she didn't show up for class, and when I phoned to follow up, Sonya told me that she was still getting a lot of headaches and felt doubtful that the program would work.

Her resignation was palpable, and I coached her for an hour on the phone, pointing out each time she would utter a "Yeah, but …" or an "I don't know." After focusing on her resistance to change and her insistence on maintaining herself as a victim, something finally clicked. Sonya returned to class the following week and brightly reported that she had stopped getting migraines altogether. I saw her two years later at a cafe and hardly recognized her. She looked great, dressed in bright colors, her skin glowing. She told me that her life had changed from the moment of our phone conversation. She still was without headaches, had gotten a job promotion, and was more fulfilled in her life than ever.

Sonya no longer saw herself as a victim of circumstance but as a designer of her life. That leap both required and created a shift in mood that was reflected in her body and her self-concept, which produced less stress and tension. She used to think that her problem was the pain in her head. When she shifted her focus to herself as a total living being, her life changed. She understood that she was not just her physical self. She was also her thoughts, feelings, and moods, which affected her life and the outlook she had about her health. She was in control.

■ ■ ■

Cultivating Beginner's Mind

In working with clients, I ask them to start over again, to become beginners. In *Zen Mind, Beginner's Mind*, Zen Master Shunryu Suzuki Roshi writes, "In the beginner's mind there are many possibilities, but in the expert's there are few." A beginner is like a new puppy: wide-eyed, all feet, no experience, but eager. It is necessary for sufferers of chronic pain to cultivate beginner's mind so that they can begin to wonder instead of worry about their problem. It is only then that they can interrupt their fears and old ways of thinking and make space for new questions and solutions to arise. They must be willing to suspend their preconceptions and see with fresh eyes.

Remember Marla, who resisted the suggestion that her over-the-counter pain preparations could be the cause of her chronic headaches? I received the following letter from her several months later, which highlights the pervasive problem of rebound headaches from medication overuse. At the same time, it illustrates beginner's mind.

As a coach, I see that Marla was able to solve the problem by suspending her old belief and taking the coaching. Of course, it helped her to finally have the information about rebound headaches. But it was only after she made the decision to investigate the possibilities that her situation completely reversed. She remains headache free five years later.

Dear Jan,

I was in your class which started in January 1997. At that time I had been taking over-the-counter (OTC) headache medication daily for about fourteen years. During your class I learned about rebound headaches. Wish someone had told me of them long ago. Since class, little by little, I've been getting off the OTC meds.

I'm happy to report that I am now in my third week of NO Excedrin—I feel like the cycle is broken. It's exciting! Not only is my head better, but I've also had NO irritable bowel syndrome, which has been a problem for many years.

Thank you for your help,

Marla

▓ ▓ ▓

Curiosity and Perseverance

If beginner's mind is about being open, then curiosity and perseverance are what keep us going. Imagine having the curiosity of a detective, endlessly tracking down leads, following each trail until it runs cold, then on to the next, and on and on. This approach to headache management requires that clients get curious about the relationship between their headaches and what's going on in their lives. I break it up into areas like diet, environment, lifestyle, and physical, hormonal, and medication factors. I ask, for example, what is the connection between your migraines and what you ate or didn't eat today? How do your tension headaches and current stress and pain levels relate? Can you feel your shoulders?

Perseverance calls us to stay on the path, even when it's rough and rocky, and to keep coming back to it when we stray. When we start feeling better and begin to resume our regular schedule, we need to be consistent in maintaining the behavior that made us feel better in the first place. With curiosity and perseverance, patients can make the connection between the behavior and the outcome. At first, Marla could not see the connection between her migraines and her Excedrin, so she continued to use it. Once she made the connection, she could change to more supportive, healthy practices and gradually eliminate it.

■ ■ ■

Always Practicing Something

Author and aikido master George Leonard observes, "We are always practicing something." Carol, a young adult with a budding sales career, maintained her busy schedule on a diet of five colas a day. Whether she acknowledged it or not, she was practicing a cola diet, which resulted in rebound headaches from caffeine, sugar, high stress, and lack of real food. She finally got off the cola, committed to eating a healthier diet, and began taking time for herself. By changing her practices, she conquered her headaches.

Cultivating regular somatic practices that support health and well-being can help people return to the lived experience of the body. For example, breathing, vipassana meditation, chi gung, and regular exercise can help build one's capacity to be conscious in the moment. By calming the mind and returning to the body over and over again, people can even change their biochemistry, lower their heart rate, respiration, and blood pressure, and reduce their pain. In addition to helping people gain a deeper awareness of their body's experiences and needs, somatic practices give people somewhere to keep returning, and allow them to begin relaxing in their own skin.

■ ■ ■

Working with Pain

Somatic self-care asks people to work with their pain. This means that they bring their attention and touch right into the site of their pain, tension, or tightness. They feel and work with their bodily sensations instead of trying to flee them. How does that tension in your shoulder feel? When and how did it begin? What shape and size is it? Does it burn? Feel numb? Does the pain move or stay in one place? We can use our pain as a signpost to direct us to the place that needs work.

Once the awareness is present, people can use touch to effectively diffuse and relieve their pain. Remember when you were a child and bumped your knee and your mother told you, "Rub it, and it will feel better"? This highly effective pain-relief measure—touch—is a sadly forgotten part of traditional pain management, but when used skillfully it can halt pain in its tracks. For example, if your left shoulder is painful, you can apply touch to explore the qualities of that pain: Is it hot, cold, hard, like a knot, or like a metal plate? How deep and wide is that knot? Then you can begin to match that "outer" touch to your "inner" pain sensations. Similar to people in certain Arctic regions who have many words that describe varieties of snow, you can learn to feel subtle distinctions of tissue. You can read its quality, then use the appropriate touch to soften it, melt it, and dissolve your pain. With practice, clients employing a somatic approach learn to master the subtleties of touch.

■ ■ ■

Headaches As a Key to Other Doors

When we explore our headaches with beginner's mind, we discover ever deeper and subtler layers of our conditioned responses that affect other aspects of our lives as well. We originally learned how to deal with pain in our families and our environment; this learning also influences our experience of pain. Awareness of embodied, conditioned responses can provide a key to unwinding our patterns of non-self-care. A whole new vista opens for people when they begin to experience how their thoughts, worries, fears, and anxieties directly affect the tension and holding in their body, breath, and mood, and how the combination contributes to their headaches. They learn to observe and shift their mind, musculature, breath, posture, and expression and thus stop the cycle. It is the consciousness of how they are affected that empowers people to make and sustain change.

After seven private sessions Stephanie, a successful yet modest professional, had the basic Mundo Program under her belt. She had reduced her black tea consumption from six to two cups a day. She was eating a balanced, healthy diet, doing her daily centered breathing practice, and even exercising. Remarkably, her daily intake of Imitrex, Midrin, and butalbital was now down to an occasional Tylenol. As a result of everything she was doing, Stephanie was having seventy-five percent fewer migraines, or one a week, and they lasted for less than a day instead of days at a time.

Despite her progress, she came into her session distressed and at a loss as to what caused her latest bout. I coached Stephanie to keep returning her attention to her activities before the headache's onset. She said that she was trying to "get her list of things done," so she ignored her body's signals to pee during her entire exercise walk. As we talked, she saw that she routinely holds her body tight when she is "just trying to get every-thing done." She recognized the "tape loops" in her head as variations of feeling guilty and denying her most basic needs. Consciously, she wanted to create better health and well-being for herself.

As Stephanie explored how and where she learned to deny and feel guilty about her needs, she recounted childhood experiences. Her mother disapprovingly characterized people who pay attention to themselves as self-indulgent. Exploring this perspective was instrumental in helping Stephanie make the connection between her childhood conditioning and how she lived her present life. She saw the pressures she put on herself, and the resulting tension held in her body that contributed to her migraines. When people reach this understanding, real change begins to takes place in many domains of their lives.

■ ■ ■

To the Future: After the Pain Is Gone

In committing one's daily activities to the whole-person approach, the headache student arrives in new territory. After a life that has revolved around pain, what does pain-free feel like? People typically respond in one of two ways: "This is great. I can finally enjoy my life!" or "How do I design my life now?" No matter what the response, the key to continued success is in maintaining basic practices. As years of tension, fear, and worry melt away, people have more time and energy available for enjoyable and productive pursuits. Life doesn't have to be carved out around head-aches anymore.

In somatic self-care, people are asserting their power to heal them-selves, rather than just suffering. They are reducing the intensity and fre-quency of their headaches, and feeling more in control of them, their health, and their life. As a result, they can spend more time with family and friends, miss fewer workdays, and experience an increase in their overall sense of well-being. With their symptoms as teacher, they are learning how their body works, and how to work with it. In doing so, they are able to move beyond their headaches to claim and redirect their destiny.

▨ Notes

1. X. H. Hu, L. E. Markson, R. B. Lipton, W. F. Stewart, and M. L. Berger, "Burden of migraine in the United States: Disability and economic costs," *Archives of Internal Medicine* 159, no. 8 (Apr. 26, 1999): 813–18.

2. H. C. Diener, "Medication overuse," *Cephalalgia* 21, no. 4 (May 2001): 278. Conference abstracts of the 10th Congress of the International Headache Society: IHC 2001.

3. Rodolfo Low, *Victory Over Migraine* (New York: Henry Holt, 1987).

4. T. Wilson, K. Keller, F. McCloud, J. Mundo, and C. A. Lee, "The cost effectiveness of a migraine programme as contrasted to pharmacological migraine treatment," Abstract, *Cephalalgia* 21, no. 4 (May 2001): 368–69. Conference abstracts of the 10th Congress of the International Headache Society: IHC 2001.

5. R. B. Lipton and W. F. Stewart (1999), in A. M. Rapoport, "What do migraine patients want?" *Neurology Treatment Updates*, Medscape, Inc., 2000.

6. Peter L. Schnall, "Locus of control and cardiovascular health," Job Stress Network website, http://www.workhealth.org/risk/rfblocus.html, 2000.

Chapter 21

Something Happened …

∼ Michael Moran

A ccording to Jung, "If we don't suffer ourselves, then we make others suffer for us." This has certainly been true in my life. But then the question becomes how do we suffer (experience) ourselves? What processes do we go through in order to know who we are and what we want? What, in our being, tells us that we are on track, or that we are betraying something that we care about?

I have found that somatically oriented approaches offer the most effective and direct modes of helping my clients get in touch with who they are; not intellectually or objectively, not through categorical deduction or historical explanation, but through the direct, lived experience of being themselves.

As in any effective therapeutic discourse, in somatic work it is essential to begin working with clients around their fundamental concerns: the things that make their lives meaningful to them. This is often challenging, as most of the people I have worked with are not accustomed to specifying in detail their goals. They often offer very generic notions of what constitutes a good life: I want to be happier; I want to be able to assert myself more effectively; I want to be a better leader. People view what they really care about as unimportant, either because they see it as too self-centered, politically incorrect, or socially inappropriate, or because they tend to hold themselves and their thoughts as relatively unimportant in general.

During early sessions of somatic work I help clients dig deep into what lies underneath their desires. What are the fundamental values that guide actions? What are their competencies or limitations at this point in life? How is their worldview expressed in their actions? Is that worldview appropriate for who they say they are or not? It is through this kind of exploration that we come to the goals that we want to achieve through our work together and to the criteria for success.

One of the things that makes somatic bodywork unusually effective is its offer of a way into the self that is not filtered through culture or psychology. When allowed to, the body expresses itself through direct experience. Clients find themselves being deeply authentic without prologue or setup. One result of this process is that clients often see results of somatic work in areas of their lives where they did not expect it. I have found it to be frustrating to have a client notice very little during a bodywork session only to report at the next session that some important part of life had changed significantly since we had last met. The client may have become more open with new people, bolder in conversations with family members, or more appropriately assertive at the office. It is often difficult for a new client to imagine that a change in the ability to experience sensations in the moment will result in a change in the ability to produce desirable life changes.

On several occasions I have had clients walk away from a session early in our work together with an attitude that seemed to express a sort of tolerant amusement at the somatic coaching process. They would graciously thank me for the experience while unable to state clearly why they were thanking me. For a somatic practitioner to hear a client express confusion or disorganization at the end of a session is good news; there are openings for new interpretations in certain disorienting states. Such clients, however, may not be so optimistic during those moments. Later, they may come in and tell stories that illuminate how somatic changes express themselves in their lives. They usually begin by saying, "Something different happened …"

On one occasion a man in his late forties came to me because he was recently jarred by his girlfriend of one year who told him that she was moving out of his life without being able to explain exactly why. He was clearly shaken; his eyes had a startled, darting quality, muscles in his face had an uncomfortable, pinched look, his head was slightly bowed, and his shoulders hung forward and down with a distinct sense of resignation. Energetically, he looked as if he were hanging by a chain attached somewhere between his shoulder blades. I suggested that he might be able to think more clearly if he were to get in touch with his body through some bodywork. He stated that he was willing to try.

He came in for one session in which I took a basic approach, assisting him to explore how his body tended to react to a sense of betrayal and shock. The session itself was uneventful. We worked on his breathing by bringing his attention to how his breath filled his upper chest and how his diaphragm and stomach did not seem to coordinate well with the breath entering his chest. We also worked on allowing his shoulders to loosen across his chest and between his shoulder blades. I noticed that, as he began to loosen and relax in his upper body and shoulders, his mood shifted away from offense and bewilderment toward more centered self-acceptance. He began to face himself with more compassion and understanding. This allowed him to begin to open up to a wider range of possible avenues for thought. He began to build his ability to empathize with his partner even though he maintained his resentment of her actions.

At the end of the session we discussed some new ways of thinking about his situation. In his mind not much had changed. Although I could see significant changes in his breathing, posture, and symmetry, I could tell that he was expecting something more, or different, from our work. He thanked me for the session and told me he would get back to me about further work.

I ran into him later the following week and asked him about anything that might have changed following our session. He looked somewhat puzzled and then reported that he felt a little calmer in general, but that nothing else occurred to him. I then asked him about his relationship. He said, with some excitement, "Oh, a day or so after I saw you we sat down and had an incredible conversation. We talked about things that I have wanted to talk about for months. And I was able to say things that I have been afraid to say in the past." The way he spoke I could tell that he was not connecting our work together with the quality of the conversation he had with his girlfriend. I then asked him about the mood of the conversation: adversarial? friendly? He told me that it went very smoothly. Although it didn't really resolve anything at that time, he saw it as an opportunity to discuss topics that had been too uncomfortable for each of them in the past. I asked him how he explained that the conversation came about when it did. He said that he wasn't sure; "maybe it was just timing."

I have found this to be a fairly typical response from people who are just "trying out" somatic bodywork. They don't engage in it consistently enough to begin to see the relationship between getting in touch with the experience of living fully in their bodies and their ability to increase their effectiveness in producing the kinds of lives they want to have. There was no reason for this man to see the connection given his background experiences. His frame of reference was looking at his external world and trying to "figure it out," as is the case for most people in our culture. He was not oriented toward a somatic perspective.

A woman came to me who was struggling to get out of a long-term marriage that she was starting to see as undermining her self-esteem and dignity. She was from an Asian culture in which women were expected to play a tolerant and subservient role in a marriage. After living in America for many years, her tolerance level had shifting and been exceeded. She presented with a gentle, deferential, and accommodating posture, tender voice, and impeccable etiquette.

Throughout our time together she would have great difficulty responding to my questions about her experiences in sensation. She would clearly search for body references but would tend to end up frustrated. We would work on her breathing, examining the relationship between the effort it took to keep her breathing shallow and the difficulty she experienced in asserting herself. I suggested some postural changes, which allowed her to see how she might have been perceived or dismissed by others and how she could turn that around. We engaged in interactive movement designed to bring forth a new way of experiencing and understanding how sensation and mood affected her relationships in real time. We connected the way she used language to the way she moved in her body. We also did some energetically oriented bodywork. We focused on her tendencies to armor herself in certain ways, particularly in her jaw and neck areas, and worked to increase her ability to tolerate the sensations that inevitably arise when armoring begins to soften.

As is often the case, I was able to see subtle changes occurring in her that she had trouble identifying. She had a tendency to think that whatever she was noticing, she was probably supposed to notice something else, something more significant. Over time she did notice that her behavior with her husband was changing. This was both good and bad news. On the one hand, she was not tolerating his verbal abuse as much as she had. On the other hand, as she began to get in touch with her toleration level, she became somewhat uncomfortable in that she began to feel the effects of the unacceptable behavior more deeply. In her case, this resulted in a feeling of being trapped, even as her husband began to respond positively to her new ability to assert herself. Her ability to feel the pain of his abusive behavior outdistanced his ability to change the behavior.

At one point, after she and I had been working together for several months, she and her husband went to a gathering of his family in another city. We had never discussed her relationship with her in-laws. It turns out that there was a long history of subtly abusive behavior directed at her by most of his relatives. Her husband rarely, if ever, stood up for her. Again, given their cultural background, she tended to overlook the slights and pretend that they did not bother her. On this particular occasion she found herself at the large dining table, as usual being subtly demeaned in one way or another by several family members. Without thinking about it, she very calmly stated to all at the table that she did not appreciate the way they were speaking and that she would not put up with it any longer. She said that she got a lot of wide-eyed stares from members of the family, including her husband. She noticed that she did not feel the kind of extreme discomfort that she would have expected to feel in the past if she had made such a statement. When they were leaving the party her husband asked, with some pride, "Where the hell did *that* come from? You certainly surprised them." She was puzzled by his reaction because her comment had not caused her the distress she still expected from self-assertive behavior.

When I asked her about her experience in our next session, she was still not seeing it in relation to her personal history; she was seeing it through her experience at the time, which she still found unremarkable. As we began to put the event into perspective she began to see how far outside her historical way of being her comments at the dinner table were. We talked about how, when changes occur on a somatic level, the conscious mind may be oblivious to them. This is the essence of embodiment; we *become* the qualities or skills that we seek rather than merely mimicking or emulating them.

■ ■ ■

After her remarriage a bubbly and gregarious woman in her early fifties came to me for somatic work. She was experiencing a series of profound identity changes relating to her family of origin, her relationships with an ex-husband and their children, and her spiritual and philosophical orientation, as well as her career path.

She had a history of molestation by her father over a period of several years in her childhood and early adolescence. As is often the case, there was no one in her family she felt she could trust and so she was left to cope with her betrayal and violation on her own. Her family of origin tended to be more preoccupied with appearances than relationships and, as a child, she found herself often seeking out secret places where she could read or fantasize by herself.

When she first came to me she wore her well-practiced "happy face"; broad, beautiful smile, squinting eyes lightly turned up at the corners, energy forward, hearty laugh at the ready. In session she would tend to let one thought lead to another, often without any particular intention toward resolution. I gently and repeatedly brought her back to topics relevant to our purpose. Given the nature of her background I chose not to move into bodywork too quickly. I introduced some of the concepts in conversation during several sessions. I also worked with her standing or seated in order to get her familiar with some of the basic experiences of somatic work. We would practice bringing her attention to her breath and note how changes in her breathing would produce changes in her mood and her sense of self. By paying attention to areas around her shoulders, shoulder blades, jaw, and neck she began to see how much energy she was using to maintain a rigid posture. When I felt that I had established enough rapport and trust between us, I suggested that we try some more focused somatic work. She agreed and we began.

What began as a basic session turned into a very deep experience for her. Very quickly she began to experience intense feelings and memories of events involving her father and her previous husband. The feelings of betrayal and outrage came forth as painful sobs and contractions in the front of her torso that led her to move toward a fetal position. She wrestled with contradictory impressions of rage at her father and her habitual tendency to see herself as deserving of the treatment she experienced. This is not unusual. I responded to her reactions by maintaining my own sense of groundedness and calm through my breath and my own sensate awareness. I would gently bring her back into the room and away from the practiced internal reality that she was so familiar with. For too many people, one of the hardest experiences to endure is that of deeply experiencing themselves as essentially good and valid. For many, this brings up the possibility that they have always been good and their thoughts always valid, thus undermining any notions that they ever deserved the kinds of treatment they endured. This can be very difficult to accept.

We brought the session to a close by bringing her back into the room with her sight, her hearing, and her physical sensations in the moment. We then took a few minutes to debrief the session. As we did this I watched her transform, as all of us do to some degree, from her more open and authentic self to her more worldly self, the one that she skillfully practiced in public. She left with a smile on her face as if nothing unusual had happened over the last hour. She said that she wanted this session to settle with her before she made another appointment.

I heard from her a few days later. She began by describing how intense our last session was and how surprised she was at the intensity. She made sure that I knew that she appreciated my efforts, as she was not one to hurt anyone's feelings. She then made a move that I considered quite courageous: she stated that she did not want to do any more bodywork with me in the near future. She did, however, want to continue to work with me, as she had seen the possibility for changes in her life that she had not imagined before. Given her historical tendency to take care of others before she took care of herself, I saw this as a step toward positive assertion without resorting to rejection or running away.

I accepted her request to resume treatment under those conditions and saw her the following week. She gave me an update on what followed our last session. She told me that many of the things that we had been discussing over the last weeks had become very clear to her in her relationships with her husband and her family. She was struck by the degree of calmness she felt in interactions that would have characteristically been very agitating. At the same time, she became haunted by memories that she had been avoiding.

She then told me something extraordinary about a subject that we had never discussed: she described nightmares that she had been having every night for the last forty years. These were not necessarily identical nightmares, but they were always thematically similar and had the same characters in them. These were very specific characters with very specific archetypal images: the bitch, the secret keeper, the good girl. They routinely spoke quite audibly through her voice when she was sleeping.

She said that in the last two weeks since our bodywork session her dreams had changed; they had begun to taper off. After about ten days they not only stopped, but the dream characters announced that they were leaving, as reported by her husband, by stating quite clearly, "You don't need us anymore; we're leaving."

I searched for a way to make sense of this process. Are these dream images locked in some energetic way in the cells of the body? Can we embody and maintain such characters in our being for forty years or more? What was it that was unlocked through the somatic practices that triggered such a change at such a deep and ingrained level?

We worked together for several weeks after this revelation. I could see her eyes gradually relax and her skin soften as she began to let our work settle into her being. She began to assert herself in new ways and to take risks in a variety of personal relationships, resulting in significant changes in her identity, both in her mind and in others'. She ultimately came to a new appreciation of values that she had suppressed for many years and began planning new directions for her career.

Over the years the inclusion of somatic work in my psychotherapy practice has allowed me to facilitate deeply relevant change in my clients quickly and effectively. Such changes are often deep and lasting. They tend to be self-generating in that the results of the new behavior, made possible through the somatic work, encourage further exploration and new experimentation.

Each step taken toward greater somatic awareness opens us up to new possibilities and new competencies. Each step brings forth essential human values that enhance all of our lives. Each step enables us to experience ourselves as we really are, in all our glory and with all of our limitations and flaws. Each session can be seen as a point of celebration for the experience of ourselves, fully expressed, in the present moment.

Part Six

The Military

Chapter 22

A Model for Decision Making for the Military Leader

~ Lt. Colonel Fred Krawchuk

uthentic and successful military decision making lives in the body. Picture a trained warrior surrounded by a group of swirling opponents. They attack, and the master stands his ground. Neither stiff nor soft, but acting with relaxed effort, the martial artist strikes, deflects, enters, and blends, using his attackers' energy to subdue their tumbling and crashing assault. A trained and practiced martial artist can do this because he has balance and integration between mind, body, and spirit. He embodies an alignment between what is important to him, his intent, and his individual actions. His outward actions show that he has the practiced capability of managing himself and his collective actions. Not only is he aware of his internal integration, but he also sees his potential opponents, allies, and the environment around him. By extending and blending with those around him, he shows that he is competent in managing relationships and coordinating with others. He does this with the spirit of service to protect, sustain, and defend life when threatened, as well as reconcile differences with others.

Martial artists offer military leaders an excellent example of how to approach decision-making preparation for uncertain conditions. Whether engaged in an explosive firefight or reconciling a swirling feud between ethnic factions, military leaders need to center and honestly face situations to maintain their balance and stand their ground. As for the martial artist, though, this is not enough. Leaders do not lead solitary lives. Their actions and decisions directly affect the lives of others. Successful leaders have to extend and take action with those people and organizations with whom they come in contact. Behind this extension lies the intent to protect and sustain life. Not looking for a fight or inventing an enemy, military leaders serve others with intent to resolve conflict and protect vital interests.

The purpose of this chapter is to introduce a holistic decision-making framework for leaders to use to help develop themselves and others to act decisively in an environment of uncertainty. In order to decide pragmatically and effectively, leaders need practices that will help them respond appropriately to a given situation. When faced with a demanding decision, leaders need to center themselves, face and assess the situation, develop an action plan, take decisive action and blend, learn from their actions, and then enter the decision cycle again. As with any other skill, diligent practice of this framework will improve a leader's ability to make difficult decisions under stressful conditions.

■ ■ ■

Center

Before a martial artist or leader can make a powerful move to protect and sustain the lives of others, he must have a sense of balance and self—a sense of center. If not, he may fall or be easily knocked off course. Leaders need to develop and maintain a power base of inner strength in order to thrive and sustain growth in a world of stress, conflict, and changing circumstances. Before a leader mobilizes resources and makes decisions that affect the lives of others, he needs to ensure he moves from a solid base of known values and sincere intent.

Part of this power base is physical. A decisive leader needs to develop his physical capacity for leadership. Physically, leaders need to be able to handle stress, changing circumstances, and other challenging obstacles. Physical and mental stamina are equally important. Dr. Jim Loehr, a renowned sports psychologist and writer, has worked with world-class athletes, business executives, pilots, and FBI SWAT teams to greatly enhance their performance. According to Dr. Loehr, "if you quickly experience physical fatigue, you'll quickly tire mentally and emotionally as well … [therefore] actively seeking exposure to stress through exercise can deepen your stress capacity."[1] Just like the martial artist who takes an occasional hit, a military leader must be able to handle physical and psychological danger. To step in harm's way in order to protect others requires physical preparation. Having a physical practice, then, becomes important in developing the body or vessel of a military leader.

In addition to physical practices, leaders require mental practices to help build their capacity to make difficult decisions. Mentally, leaders need to have self-knowledge and vision. Leaders are like a compass, providing direction along a determined path. To be able to do that, leaders must have their own purpose. They have to know what is important to them and know where they stand. The importance of this cannot be underestimated. George Bernard Shaw wrote:

> This is the true joy of life, the being used for a purpose recognized by yourself as a mighty one … the being a force of nature instead of a feverish, selfish little clod of ailments and grievances complaining that the world will not devote itself to making you happy.[2]

Leaders need to understand their internal true north in order to be effective. This constant bearing will consistently provide authentic direction. All actions originate from this place. Without this kind of solid reference, the leader as well as her followers will veer off course.

In order to better understand what her true north is, a leader needs to engage in those kinds of activities that demand honest self-reflection. Before leaders can develop fitting strategies and help guide an organization and its people forward, they need to know what is critical to themselves, their teams, and their personnel. They should clarify what is important and always ask themselves if they are making decisions in concert with their values and purpose.

To have a better sense of values and purpose, leaders need to occasionally reflect on such questions as:

- You have only two years to live and will do so with your health intact. What will you do with your remaining time? With whom, where, and why?

- You have just won the lottery. What will you do with the rest of your life? With whom, where, and why?

- Write a letter now imagining that you are on your deathbed. What did you accomplish? What was important to you? Where and with whom did you have an impact?

- What is most needed in the world?

The practice of self-reflection of a leader's heartfelt desires and concerns helps develop a powerful base of balance and direction. By understanding her true north, a leader has a better sense of what is important to her and where to focus her attention. This will help a leader find the best places for her to be in the flow and thereby more authentically offer her service. This type of awareness will help leaders find the best organizations and assignments suited to their needs and capabilities. This, in turn, will help leaders declare the values and principles of the units they lead. When a leader establishes well-understood organizational priorities, and these are aligned with her own values and actions, she will create a simple elegance of harmony and trust that creates efficiency in how the organization operates.

To ensure organizational alignment, leaders need to take time on a regular basis to conduct an "azimuth check," a regular review of goals and priorities. Just as they individually check their own compasses, they must do the same with their organizations. Soldiers want to make a difference and need to know that their efforts count. Looking back at their service, they want to know that their sacrifices, intense training and long deployments were worth it, that it all had meaning. Leaders have to take time, then, to ensure that their units are on track and that they are creating meaning for their personnel.

An azimuth check will help focus soldiers and give their work meaning, especially in times of crisis. I learned about azimuth checks from Brigadier General Stan McChrystal, a former 75th Ranger Regimental Commander, now Chief of Staff of the 18th Airborne Corps. The azimuth check ensures a common vision for current and incoming leaders by summarizing what the unit has accomplished during the past year (and what it learned from the efforts), an assessment of the current status of the unit, and a clear, focused direction for where it will go from here. It serves as both a contract between leaders on where they hope to go and a yardstick to measure their progress.

For many leaders, a sense of service is an important centering value in azimuth checks and decision making. Meaningful military leadership requires an attitude of care and service that protects and sustains life. This sense of selfless service is the linchpin that binds values and decisions together and gives them dignity and responsibility. Military leaders make decisions that directly influence the lives of others. Therefore, a sense of responsibility is imperative. Authentic military leadership exists only when it is carried out in service to others for the sake of protecting lives and vital interests.

This sense of care and service needs to be practiced and embodied, just as the other competencies of leadership. A leader must approach all of his tasks with a sense of service. In the background of his actions, a leader reminds himself that everything he does, he does for the sake of protecting lives and defending the Constitution. This attitude in mind, he embodies the knowledge that:

Every action taken, from the moment we switch off the alarm clock in the morning to the way we write ... design a product ... [train or counsel a soldier], has the potential to change the world, leave it cold with indifference, or perhaps, more commonly, nudge it infinitesimally in the direction of good and evil.[3]

Leaders who practice service know that there is no such thing as a trivial decision. Poor leaders may trivialize decisions, but authentic leaders know that whatever they say or do not say, do or do not do, has an impact. That is why they care about developing decision-making competencies that align them with a sense of service. Caring, authentic leaders practice moving through the world with purposeful intent and thoughtful action, knowing that they embody the warrior's ethos to protect, defend, and sustain lives.

■ ■ ■

Face and Assess the Situation

With an understanding of center and one's core values, we will look at how leaders need to face and assess situations honestly. To be effective in decision making requires having the best information available to make a solid decision. The leader must gather pertinent facts and information in order to define the problem or opportunity in front of him before he can make a decision. Therefore, situational awareness is critical to having as complete a picture as feasible of a given situation.

Facing a situation means lining up to it directly and openly. An effective leader does not misjudge what is in front of him; he observes what is unfolding in front of him and reports it accurately. He allows for new possibilities and a possible initial lack of clarity. He looks into the fog as an opportunity to shape his reality in terms of his values and end state.

Always aware of his center and long-term vision, he observes the present moment with clear concentration. "Being able to maintain a sharp focus and broad comprehension simultaneously is one of the most important qualities for leadership effectiveness."[4] Being present sets up the leader for successful decision making. Being open and aware, a mindful leader makes the best use of the information available to him, which directly impacts the quality of his decision.

Leaders need to observe exactly what they observe, not what they think they are supposed to observe. They need to assess situations based on what they think, feel, and understand, not what they think they are supposed to think, feel, or understand. Leaders have to ensure that those they lead are not encouraged to report only good news to the boss. Leaders need to create an open, trusting environment in which people can report information truthfully and not face negative consequences for bringing in bad news or surprises.

For effective decision making, a leader needs to have a calm mind and be able to focus. Effective leaders are the calm in the storm and stay focused under pressure. Like snipers who practice breath control and relaxation techniques in order to take critical shots under pressure, military leaders need similar practices. This is especially true since they successfully lead by being a container for potentially disruptive emotions and must exercise self-control. Like self-knowledge, self-control demands practice.

A regular meditation practice can help. Meditation training allows leaders to develop the centered, present moment awareness to "become now-focused like a professional athlete with single-minded devotion to a task in the midst of dynamic circumstances."[5] Many scientific studies clearly show that meditation can help people achieve calmness and focus. These well-documented experiments unquestionably demonstrate that meditation helps heighten perception, improves responses to stress, and improves concentration and attention.[6] Dr. Jim Loehr prescribes meditation to his clients because it helps strengthen the "capacity for ... calmness of the mind and precise concentration."[7] The empirical evidence is clear that these practices can have a powerful effect on a leader's ability to be composed and centered, which, in turn, plays an important role in accurately assessing situations and making appropriate decisions.

■ ■ ■

Develop an Action Plan and Extend

Once a leader accurately assesses a situation, then she can extend and develop an action plan. One way of exercising the mind and practicing developing action plans is to look at how different people make decisions and the variety of analytical tools available. In order to develop an action plan, one should structure the situation a leader faces. A successful decision maker clearly understands the problem or opportunity she faces and the reasons behind the present situation. With a clear definition of the problem and where she wants to go, she can then look at different criteria for weighing her alternatives, options, and possible outcomes.

Different professions offer a variety of effective ways of structuring problems and decisions. Many graduate programs offer the case study method. John Boyd, an influential military thinker and strategist, taught fighter pilots and military decision makers the importance of observation-orientation-decision-action (the OODA loop).[8] Martial arts training also offers an active way of learning to quickly assess a situation, develop an action plan, and receive instantaneous feedback on one's decisions. This approach helps people learn to think on their feet. According to Morgan Jones, former CIA analyst and author of a book on problem solving, there "is a veritable armory of ... weapons with which to survey, probe, dissect, diagnose, and resolve every kind of problem from the simplest to the most complex and foreboding."[9] Practicing martial arts, analyzing news events using different structural tools, and practicing decision making on case studies and daily situations are but a few ways leaders can actively develop their abilities to solve problems and make good decisions. What is important is to practice structuring problems, analyzing decisions in a logical way, and fully considering alternatives.

■ ■ ■

Take Decisive Action and Blend

After a leader extends his action plan to others, he then makes a decision and blends with the situation. Embodying the ability to work effectively with people becomes an essential leadership competency. What are some of the practices military professionals can undertake to develop and maintain this capacity? A look at effective martial arts, successful sports teams, cohesive military units, and successful negotiators sheds important light on beneficial practices.

Aikido is an effective and practical Japanese martial art that stresses harmony. Aikido offers its students "the ability to blend, both physically and mentally, with the movement and energy of [their] partner[s] ... [It is] the study of good communication."[10] Practitioners of this discipline look at ways of using the opponent's forces against himself. Forcing and straining is futile. Aikido teaches students to maintain their stand, coordinate with multiple opponents, and maintain a sense of dignity for themselves and others.

I have trained soldiers, teachers, lawyers, and counselors in simple aikido movements to help them actively coordinate, resolve conflicts, and develop cohesive teams. My students do not just talk or think about these concerns. Being physically active learners, they gain a deeper understanding of leadership and the concept of flow. For leaders already competent in conflict resolution and developing teams, this training offers a complementary cross-training advantage.

Introducing martial arts or combatives training as part of the leadership development for crisis action planning has other advantages as well. When faced with conflict in a crisis action environment, a leader needs more options than simply fight or flee. In defense of vital interests, a decision maker may need to employ lethal force. At other times, when facing an emotionally charged situation that does not directly impact the mission, simply walking away may be the best course of action. Given the often hazy environment of a crisis, other options are needed. Competent and practical combatives training offers a third way to deal with force. By blending with an opponent, a leader keeps his interests intact, sees the antagonist's perspective, and then applies an appropriate amount of nonlethal force that resolves the situation safely and effectively. This does not take years of practice. Simple moves introduced during a training period and practiced over time will give leaders confidence in themselves to resolve conflict utilizing nonlethal means without depending on only the fight or flee options.

Martial arts training also helps people deal more effectively not only with others, but also with themselves. Some soldiers are more aggressive than others. Combatives training will allow overly aggressive soldiers who are quick to use force a way of channeling their energy in a more constructive manner when facing conflict. Combatives training will also provide additional tools to passive soldiers who might be more apt to avoid or withdraw from a hot dispute. Skillful combatives training, then, can help soldiers, depending on their personality, contain their aggression or open up appropriate responses in order to more safely and decisively handle a situation.

In preparing soldiers for deployments to the Balkans, we would run uncertain scenarios for soldiers to help them develop the capacity to think on their feet and make quick decisions. In one instance, armed thugs confronted our soldiers. Those that had gone through a combatives course quickly disarmed the threat that interfered with the mission using nonlethal means and secured the objective. Another group of soldiers who had not gone through combatives training involved themselves in a shouting match with the thugs; tensions rose and a shoot-out ensued, leaving one American soldier dead and the threat forces dispersed.

To help improve their organization's performance and improve decision making, leaders must set up the conditions for flow states of optimal kinesthetic performance. To do this, leaders must ensure that "goals are clear, feedback relevant, and challenges and skills are in balance" so that "attention becomes ordered and fully invested."[11] This kind of focused training allows concentration to overcome self-consciousness because there is no room for distracting thoughts. To actualize this concept, leaders need to offer clear standards, teach proper techniques, allow time for practice, and coach along the way. Rehearsing critical events with essential players should become a standard operating procedure. Planning, brainstorming without evaluation, modeling, and simulations help teams build a creative learning process that leads to successful decisions.

■ ■ ■

Learn and Enter the Decision-Making Loop Again

Decision making is an ongoing process. Once a decision is made and implemented, actions taken will have an impact, some predicted, others not. Being aware of the feedback, learning from the unfolding interactions with the environment, and applying lessons learned to the next decision cycle will make for surer and smarter decisions in the future.

One way of learning from the decision-making process is to have a practice of coaching. Tied to the individual and organizational practice of sustained learning, providing and receiving feedback on a regular basis is a practical and beneficial way to practice integrity, in addition to the added benefit of professional development. Coaching, when done correctly, provides an opportunity for leaders to deal directly with their team members and maintain open lines of communication. By taking the time to coun-sel their people on a regular basis, leaders offer a clear example of care and concern for their welfare and development. Since professional devel-opment is important to a leader's vision, actively engaging in it and pro-moting it builds credibility.

Coaching or performance counseling does not have to be only verbal. Military leaders can make counseling interesting and impactful by exam-ples of embodied behavior. Applying basic moves such as centering and blending from aikido can help leaders better understand and experience embodied behavior.

During performance counseling with my subordinate leaders, I used simple moves to help show them how they came across in stressful situa-tions. Special Forces soldiers do not generally have a problem being direct, and they typically do not back away or avoid conflicts. Therefore, I helped them to see how to approach conflict from other angles while still main-taining their balance and interests by demonstrating centering and then executing blending moves.

In one example of this counseling, I noticed that one of my men went to his head when situations started to heat up. He would lose his cool and unnerve his co-workers. As we did centering and blending exercises, I would ask him to feel the ground under his feet, to feel connected to the earth. Every time he went up in his head, became physically top-heavy, and lost his balance, I redirected his attention to his feet. Eventually he learned to feel his feet on the ground whenever he encountered a stressful situation that could potentially throw him off balance.

As my leaders progressed with this training I introduced wooden swords into the practice. The sword represented an extension of embodied behav-iors. One captain had a tendency to make the same point repeatedly and would not let go of his argument. This overkill made it harder for others to listen to him. I gave him the sword and asked him to make a cut while stating one of his arguments. Then I introduced my sword, which repre-sented the environment and others participating in the argument. As we made contact he would incessantly follow me around the room. I even laid down my sword and went to my computer, purposely ignoring him, and he still followed me, not letting go. Finally it dawned on him that although he made his point early in the exchange, he had the habit of continually pressing his arguments, ultimately turning people off with his stubborn behavior.

Another example demonstrated the importance of staying focused on one's intent and carrying through with one's decision. Having stated his intent and purpose clearly, and making a clean and forceful move, another captain came toward me with his sword. Instead of blocking or counterattacking, I let him go by me, ignoring his move. This surprised him. Instead of maintaining his movement and carrying through with the cut, he became caught up in my reaction and lost his balance. Later, when we discussed the exercise, he said he became frustrated with my response to his move. He felt that he had "done everything right" and so I should have responded appropriately. I explained that even when we make correct, well-thought-out decisions, we would encounter obstacles, disagreement, and even people ignoring our moves in the world.

The important lesson from this embodied exercise is to remember to stay focused on one's sincere intent and keep moving to the best of one's ability in order to carry out the decision. Decision makers should not seek the approval of others; thus, they cannot afford to get caught up in the reactions of others. Instead of looking for recognition or praise, effective decision makers make skillful decisions because that is the right thing to do.

By learning kinesthetically and observing themselves in action, military leaders have an opportunity to embody appropriate decision-making behaviors. The practice of movement, especially with partners, vividly helps show embodied behavior and deepens learning. This kind of counseling is not simply an intellectual exercise or verbal exchange. Embodied coaching is alive and real for all involved. It takes learning from the head into the body, where muscle memory is developed for future conflict resolution and decision making.

■ ■ ■

Conclusion

A considerable body of knowledge is available on leadership and decision making. This knowledge is important and necessary. However, leaders need to go a step further and embody this knowledge, like any other successful professional who has mastered his art, in order to be effective. Military leaders, like martial artists, need practices that will help them stay on the path of self-knowledge, inner strength, and personal mastery of decision-making skills. Embodied decision-making practices will allow leaders to build the character they need to effectively assess and act and not lose themselves to the pressure of the situation. Like athletes dedicated to team sports, leaders need practices that help them develop the capacity to make appropriate decisions with, through, and for people.

Military leaders must dedicate themselves to lifelong practices that are based on a value system, involve their whole person, and are guided by coaches. The notion of leadership as a service to others provides the linchpin that brings purpose of decision making and leadership together. Close examination and implementation of physical, mental, and kinesthetic interpersonal practices will lead to beneficial results for organizations and the embodiment of thoughtful action in decision makers. Like the martial arts master who deftly handles a multiple attack, the leader in a fast-moving and fluid environment, with proper leadership development, learns to adapt to any given situation. Authentic military leaders, through embodied practices, become "as hard as a diamond, flexible as a willow, smooth-flowing like water or as empty as space" in order to make the right decisions that lead their organizations to victory.[12]

■ Notes

1. James Loehr, *Stress for Success* (New York: Random House, 1997).
2. George Bernard Shaw, *Man and Superman* (New York: Penguin, 1950), preface.

3. David Whyte, *The Heart Aroused: Poetry and the Preservation of Soul in Corporate America* (New York: Doubleday, 1994), p. 265.

4. Kevin Cashman, *Leadership from the Inside Out: Becoming a Leader for Life* (Provo, Utah: Executive Excellence Publishing, 1998), p. 93.

5. Ibid., p. 90.

6. Michael Murphy, *The Future of the Body* (Los Angeles; Tarcher, 1992), pp. 603–11.

7. Loehr, *Stress for Success*, p. 129.

8. Grant Hammond, *The Mind of War: John Boyd and American Security.* (Washington, D.C.: Smithsonian Institution, 2001), p. 190.

9. Morgan D. Jones, *The Thinker's Toolkit: 14 Powerful Techniques for Problem Solving* (New York: Times Books, 1998), p. 309.

10. Mitsugi Saotome, *The Principles of Aikido* (Boston: Shambala Publications, 1989), p. 9.

11. Mihaly Csikszentmihalyi, *Finding Flow: The Psychology of Engagement with Everyday Life* (New York: Basic Books, 1997), p. 31.

12. Morihei Ueshiba, founder of aikido.

Chapter 23

A Lesson in Fear

~ Capt. John Duvall, USMC

Corporal Patrick Bishop was from Humbolt County in northern California. A big, ruddy-faced kid with a quick temper and a gruff demeanor, Corporal Bishop was respected but at the same time feared by the other Marines in my platoon. He was one of three squad leaders in the platoon, but at the same time he took it upon himself to look after all those Marines in the platoon at his rank or below. He did this by two methods: by intimidation and by example, two completely opposed forms of leadership. The reasons they worked were, one, Bishop was a large, imposing individual, and two, he generally wanted to do the right thing. He had the Marines' and the platoon's best interest at heart. And those individual Marines in the platoon who were lazy, or tired, or who bitched and moaned when things got tough received no sympathy from Corporal Bishop: they got a face-to-face ass chewing from the 220-pound former big-timber lumberjack. Yes, he was quick-tempered and lacked tact in certain situations, but I could count on him to get the job done in exigent circumstances. His leadership style was risky. It was effective, but there was the possibility that it could kill morale. It was a fine line, and I had to be sure he walked it.

When I took command of the platoon, I had a lot of work to do, not necessarily to correct any deficiencies the platoon might have, but to earn their respect. Platoon commanders, in the eyes of the Marines of the platoon, are temporary. They are the weakest link when they first take command. Many of the Marines in the platoon had been there three, four, or even five years and were "salty." A new lieutenant stepping into the platoon represented just another "boot" to train and teach. Yes, you were the commander and, yes, the Marines executed the proper customs and courtesies toward you, but that was because they were Marines and they were professional, not because they respected you. Respect was something that you had to earn, and the Marines did not give it to you easily, especially to Corporal Bishop.

Marines gain respect for their leaders by observing three things: 1) the way in which you conduct yourself as their leader (leadership by example), 2) the way in which you deal with problems in the platoon (fairness), and 3) your ability to exude coolness under fire (showing no fear).

Leading by example is the most obvious way to lead Marines. If you eat before your Marines, go to sleep before your Marines, wake up after your Marines, or fall out of a run or hike in front of your Marines, your effectiveness and credibility as their leader is nil. They must have absolute confidence that you can do things as well as they can, at a minimum. It is far better to exceed their levels of proficiency. It inspires confidence.

Fairness requires moral courage. It is easy to punish the individual who is always doing something wrong. You come to expect it from them. It is much more difficult to punish the superstar who commits the same infraction. But that is what must be done. A sense of fairness has to be maintained if you desire respect from your subordinates. Play favorites and you will lose any respect that you have gained. This develops a sense of injustice and lack of confidence in the leader's ability to make any kind of decision.

As a leader, I had no difficulty demonstrating these two leadership traits. They were obvious, and for me they were easy. I had plenty of opportunities to demonstrate my proficiency and lead by example. I had been well trained in the technical aspects of my job as a combat engineer, my level of fitness was outstanding, and my uniforms were always immaculate. Fairness was another no-brainer. If done properly, fair punishment can be an outstanding motivator.

The third trait, however, the ability to show no fear, made me uneasy. The two previous traits could easily be demonstrated in a garrison and training environment. But I had never been exposed to fear in front of these Marines, and I had no idea how the Marines or I would react in that type of situation. We had our Marine training and defined leadership down to the lowest ranks. Would that be enough in a chaotic and fearful environment like combat? Would I inspire confidence in my Marines? Would I shoot or would I freeze? There is no realistic way to train for this aspect of combat. We could simulate it but never duplicate it in training. Or could we?

In early May of 2000, word came down from our chain of command that the commandant of the Marine Corps, the most senior Marine officer in our corps, was initiating a new program to develop and train Marines in martial arts. The commandant, General James L. Jones, had served with the Republic of Korea (ROK) Marines earlier in his career and was impressed with their ability in martial arts, not only as a combat tool, but also as a tool for personal discipline and physical and mental fitness. The commandant's goal was to develop and institute a similar program in the United States Marine Corps. Our battalion, 1st Combat Engineer Battalion, 1st Marine Division, was chosen to be the test unit. The wide variety of Military Occupational Specialties (MOSs) in our battalion provided a good sample of combat and combat service support Marines to test the program and ensure that it could be applied throughout the Marine Corps. But the commandant wanted this program to become more than just another weapons system. His desire was to institute this program into the culture of the Marine Corps, and he needed to ensure the program could be applied across the spectrum of subcultures in the Corps. My platoon of combat engineers was selected to form the core of the test unit. We were then augmented by other Marines from the battalion from various MOSs to number forty Marines. I was selected as the platoon commander, and another lieutenant, Lance Attaway, was chosen to be an evaluator. He would participate in the training to provide perspective and analysis on its applicability to the Corps, and I would handle command issues.

At the time the platoon was formed, the specific training regiment was unknown, as was the duration of the training and its philosophy. As time progressed, we received a training schedule with esoteric periods of instruction like "Warrior Values," "Attention Training," and "Combatives." We could only speculate as to the content. The training was to be conducted twelve to fifteen hours a day, seven days a week, for six weeks. Physical fitness training was to be conducted first thing every morning. The training consisted of long runs targeting a specific heart rate, weight training, and speed hikes (humps). Swimming sessions were also included. The first day was to consist of an indoctrination (or "indoc," as we call it) consisting of a Marine Corps Physical Fitness Test (PFT), swim qualification, combatives assessment, and a hike with full combat load. This analysis of the platoon's current state of physical fitness and motivation was to be used as a baseline for comparison to a day of exactly the same testing at the end of the six weeks.

So far everything was familiar to the Marines: running, humping, PFT, swim qual. These were the fundamentals of Marine Corps physical fitness. Then came controlled physical violence, intense fitness training sessions, and "attention" training. The most shocking and the most beneficial aspect of this training was the combatives. Combative training consisted of full-speed, full-contact fighting using specific techniques (mainly knee and elbow strikes) with a minimum of protection from the blows. The purpose of this controlled violence was four-fold: to become proficient in the techniques, to feel what it was like to get hit, to see how you would react when you were hit, and to harden the body against these blows. The training had a fifth and, for me, more important result. It brought me face to face with an act that I had encountered only once in my life and had done everything since to avoid: the fight.

My first and only "fight" happened when I was five. I was playing with a friend when two younger boys came up to us and asked if they could play with us. What exactly we were playing I cannot remember, but I do remember that we were the "bigger" boys and could not let the "little" boys join our games. The result was a challenge by my friend to the two younger boys to a fight. If they won, they could join us. Before either one of them could answer, my friend hauled off and hit one of the kids. Not to be outdone, I did the same thing to the other kid. Blood poured from his nose and he ran off crying to his house. The one thing about that incident that has stayed with me through the years was the hollow feeling I had right after I hit him. It was the first time in my life, that I can remember anyway, that I realized I had done something *wrong*. I walked home and told no one. As it turns out, I did not have to. About fifteen minutes later, the boy's father, with son in tow, showed up at our front door. My father answered, talked briefly with the father, and then shut the door. When I heard my father's footsteps coming down the hall toward my bedroom door, I was terrified. I knew what I had done was wrong, and I expected to be punished for it. My father walked into my room and sat down next to me on my bed. He could tell that I was upset and scared. He asked me what happened, and I told him. He then proceeded to explain to me the use of violence to solve problems. My father is far from a pacifist. But what I took away from that lecture was that violent action must be coupled with a sense of responsibility and accountability.

Since then, I have never been in a fight. I have been close, but I have always talked my way out of it. I was hit once by a neighborhood bully, but I didn't fight back. I talked my way out of fights or backed away from them out of fear. I was afraid to get hit. I was afraid of the pain. And here I was, at thirty years old, an officer in the United States Marine Corps, a professional warrior in one of the most revered fighting organizations in the history of warfare. And I, who had never been in a fight, was supposed to lead the Marines in my platoon into battle when ordered. How could I know if I could? When I thought about this, and believe me I thought about it often, I was ashamed. I felt like a con artist. I felt like I had betrayed the trust of my Marines and the integrity of our Corps.

Now I felt I had a shot at redemption, a chance to test myself and my Marines. Here was my chance to face the one fear that I had yet to face. And that chance came in the form of an exercise called "Bull in the Ring" and that big, ruddy-faced kid from California, Corporal Bishop.

Bull in the Ring was an exercise to test several things. It was designed to test your mastery of the combatives techniques, your aggressiveness, your ability to handle multiple opponents, and your situational awareness. But, to the Marines of the platoon, it was designed to test your toughness, your warrior spirit, and your ruthlessness. The rules were simple. All the Marines would form a circle. One Marine would enter the ring. At that point it was open season. Any number of attackers could come at you from any direction at any time. It was up to you to protect yourself.

The first time that we did this exercise I was terrified. It was not because I was afraid of the pain associated with the combatives; my body had long since grown accustomed to the physical pain. No, I was scared because I knew that Marines would be gunning for me. It was their turn to get a legal shot at the lieutenant. I knew that they would be coming at me hard in an effort to test me. And, I admit, I was scared of failing that test and letting my Marines down. The only way that I knew to overcome that fear was to apply our training: relax, "center" myself like we had been taught, focus, face the conflict (both inner and outer) consciously, react as quickly and as aggressively as I could, show methodical, skillful abandon when attacked, and keep moving. I watched in anticipation and apprehension as each Marine took his turn in the center of the ring. After about half of the Marines had taken their turn, I ran into the ring for my shot.

And that brings us back to Corporal Bishop. I had watched each Marine enter the ring to begin their bout. Bishop was always one of the first Marines to attack. I knew that as soon as I entered that ring my credibility and leadership were on the line, and he was going to be the first to test it. As it turns out, I was right. Bishop was the first to come at me. Because of his standing in the platoon as one of the enlisted leaders, he would feel that he would have to be one of the first to step up and test me. He came at me hard. I immediately went on the attack. I grabbed him around the neck and began delivering the most powerful knee strikes that I could. I threw him off as another Marine attacked. Again, I met him in an attack and continued the knee strikes. This continued for an unknown period of time with an unknown number of aggressors. All I really remember is that I completed the exercise with the respect of my Marines intact. But I had also learned an important lesson on the abatement of fear and had gained self-confidence in my abilities as a leader.

If combatives were to tone, harden, and train the body, then attention training and warrior values were to temper and still the mind. To be a true warrior and leader, one must not only be effective in a chosen discipline, but one must also have the proper mental, moral, and ethical framework from which to employ that discipline. This is the mind/body discipline of somatics. Warfare is ugly. Combat is not to be glorified. But not only is preparation for combat necessary in the profession of arms, but preparation for different types of personal "combat" is absolutely necessary for success in this world. No matter what your chosen profession you will face times of crisis, whether they are emotional, mental, spiritual, or physical. To effectively negotiate these challenges, you need to be prepared to make the right, though not necessarily the easy, choice. Doing the right thing is never easy. Many times it is unpopular. One must be focused and able to see the greater outcome to negotiate these morally ambiguous battles. This was the foundation for our body/mind training. We discussed the nature of honor, courage, commitment, and right and wrong, all set forth during our warrior values training.

While these classes on warrior values instilled sound leadership qualities, the attention training and visualization exercises developed the ability to focus the mind and remain calm under pressure, allowing for a greater sense of situational awareness, a vital quality to have on the battlefield, and in life. Attention training was basically a meditation exercise. We would relax in a sitting position and begin to focus on our breathing by counting our breaths up to five and then repeating. If you lost count, you simply acknowledged that fact and then brought yourself back to the beginning and started counting again. The goal was not to be perfect. The goal was to recognize when you were daydreaming or counting automatically in your head instead of focusing on the task at hand and bring your attention back to the breath. This exercise developed a stillness of mind allowing for greater mental focus. The ability to not be shaken by the events around you instills confidence in your subordinates and in your own abilities to make decisive, effective, and prudent decisions under duress. These qualities are applicable across the board in a unit. It improves overall combat effectiveness. Every member of a unit must be ready to assume a leadership role in the event of casualties. Attention training gives the unit a greater chance of success in this eventuality.

Our training began to develop in me something that I had never felt before in my life: an edge. It is very difficult to describe, but it has to be akin to what world-class competitive athletes attempt to develop through rigorous training. The athlete's energy level, mental focus, emotional balance, and athletic ability—a somatic sensibility—must all reach their peak on the day of competition. I could feel my body and mind hardening. A relaxed alertness took over my body and mind. My confidence was extraordinarily high, yet very quiet. To borrow an analogy from Zen Buddhism, it was as if my mind were like the stillness of a pond, not narrowly focused on any one thing but reflecting everything. This feeling and outlook affected every aspect of my life, professionally and personally. My experience was not unique. All the Marines who undertook the training reported similar results to varying degrees. Empirically, a change could definitely be identified. At the end of the six weeks the Marines were tested again, primarily by using the Marine Corps Physical Fitness Test. The scores increased an astounding twenty to thirty percent across the board. That is incredible considering the short training period of six weeks.

I carry this entire experience with me to this day, as do many of the other Marines that were involved in the program. Since that six weeks ended, my level of training has necessarily dropped off, and that edge has been dulled ever so slightly. But the effects are still with me. My leadership style and philosophy reflect the lessons learned from facing and overcoming my fear. For me this result would not have been possible without the interplay of the mind and the body. This is the science and art of somatics. I have come to learn that the mind and the body are inextricably linked, and the refinement of one necessarily affects the other. The effect is synergistic, and the result of training both in concert is greater than training each separately.

Contributors

Woody Allen, MSC, has studied business philosophy, linguistics, and leadership for over twenty-five years. He holds senior board chair positions on companies involved in broadcasting, telecommunications, and telecommunications infrastructure. Woody is president of Allen Management Services, a strategic advisory services firm based in Oakton, Virginia, and is an associate teacher with Strozzi Institute.

wallen4@cox.net

Denise Benson, MFT, is a somatic psychotherapist in private practice in Los Gatos and San Francisco, California, working with individuals, adolescents, and couples. Prior to becoming a therapist Denise wrote, developed, and taught an innovative curriculum on emotional intelligence as a junior high school teacher. She has facilitated groups as a somatic coach and is an associate at Strozzi Institute, a Master Somatic Coach, and a supervisor in the SI Somatic Coaching Program.

dkbenson@ix.netcom.com

J. Clare Bowen-Davies, M.A., is a licensed psychotherapist and Master Somatic Coach specializing in the design of programs of recovery for alcoholics and addicts in central and northern California. A recovering alcoholic herself, she brings a synthesis of experience to the recovery process which takes into account the power of the body/mind/spirit. Her commitment is to helping people in recovery live empowered lives.

www.coachinginternational.com
clare@coachinginternational.com

Patrick Clary, M.D., has been a hospice medical director since 1993. Educated at Georgetown College and Georgetown School of Medicine, he was first professionally trained in poetry as a student of Roland Flint. His poetry has been published in The New England Journal of Medicine, Journal of Medical Humanities, CoEvolution, Patient Care, and in three collections. A Quaker, he served as a medical corpsman with U.S. infantry units in combat in Vietnam from 1969 to 1970.

pclary@aol.com

Jennifer Cohen, MA, is a Master Somatic Coach who has been associated with Strozzi Institute for the past eight years. She has worked as a counselor and trainer for fourteen years, with victims of childhood sexual abuse, rape, and domestic violence. Her work is designed to facilitate growth, increase effectiveness, promote new interpretations, and create positive and lasting change.

jencohen@earthlink.net

Peter Denning, Ph.D., is a professor of computer science at the Naval Postgraduate School in Monterey, California and a Master Somatic Coach. At George Mason University he chaired the Technology Council and served as vice provost for continuing professional education, associate dean for computing, and chair of the Computer Science Department. The founding director of the Research Institute for Advanced Computer Science at NASA Ames Research Center and cofounder of CSNET, he taught computer science at Purdue, Princeton, and MIT.

pjd@nps.navy.mil

Robert Dunham founded Enterprise Performance in 1993, an executive and management company which develops skills not addressed in MBA programs or traditional management approaches. Inspired by the challenges he faced as a vice president in Motorola Computer Systems and several other companies, Robert has developed Mastering Professional Management™ and The Company of Leaders™--programs which emphasize action-generating communication skills and embodied learning.

www.enterpriseperform.com
bdunham@enterpriseperform.com

Captain John Duvall, United States Marine Corps, is currently serving at the American Embassy, Nicosia, Cyprus, as Executive Officer, Company B, Marine Security Guard Battalion, 4th Marine Expeditionary Brigade (Anti-Terrorism). He worked with Strozzi Institute on The Marine Warrior Project developing and implementing the new Marine Corps Martial Arts program.

duvalljp@hotmail.com

Lieutenant Colonel Fred Krawchuk is a U.S. Army Special Forces officer currently stationed in Fort Polk, Louisiana. He has served in a variety of leadership positions in the United States, Latin America, and Europe. Fred received a B.S. from the United States Military Academy, an M.P.A from Harvard University, and an M.B.A. from the University of Navarra–IESE, Spain. He has been a member of the Strozzi Institute community for ten years and is a Term Member with the Council on Foreign Relations. Fred's deep commitment is to global security.

fredkrawchuk@yahoo.com

Richard Leider is a founder and principal of The Inventure Group. A pioneer in career coaching, Richard is the author of The Power of Purpose and Whistle While You Work. He leads yearly Inventure Expedition walking safaris in Tanzania, East Africa, where he helped found the Dorobo Fund for youth leadership and village conservation.

www.inventuregroup.com

Paula Love, MS, is a Master NLP Programmer and counselor who works with individuals and couples to create and sustain rich relationships. She offers new interpretations and practices that support people to engage in ways they previously thought were not possible. In addition to degrees in counseling and psychology, Paula is a Master NLP Programmer and is certified as a Master Coach by the International Coach Federation and as a Master Somatic Coach by Strozzi Institute.

paula@paulaloveconsulting.com

Tom Lutes has been a teacher and coach for thirty-seven years. He has worked intimately with people from all walks of life. He and his wife Jasmine have taken their programs to many cultures around the world, including Russia, China, Japan, Malaysia, Canada, Mexico, England, and Greece.

www.stalkingtruth.com
tomlutes@starband.net

Peter Luzmore, MSC, founded Synthesis LLC in 1995, a company that enables organizations and individuals to achieve their maximum capacity to produce value for their customers, colleagues, and themselves. He is a Master Somatic Coach and has lived in London, Hong Kong, San Francisco, and New York.

pluzmore@ix.netcom.com

Michael Moran, M.A., is a licensed psychotherapist and Master Somatic Coach practicing in San Luis Obispo, California. He is committed to assisting people in discovering and clarifying their values and visions and then building their capacity to design and bring forth the lives that they want to lead. He integrates philosophical, linguistic, and psychological distinctions with an orientation to how all of these are manifested in the life of the body.

www.sanluiscounseling.com
mjmoran@charter.net

Jan Mundo, MSC, has thirty-two years experience working with the body/mind connection for chronic pain. In 1970 she developed the Mundo Method, which combines touch therapy and focused concentration to treat headaches, and the Mundo Program for holistic headache management. She is a Master Somatic Coach, massage therapist, and body-centered therapist. She is on staff at the UC San Francisco's Osher Center for Integrative Medicine. She is writing a book on headaches.

jmundo@headachehealing.com

Rich Poccia, RN, is a martial artist and registered nurse in the San Francisco Bay Area specializing in emergency medicine and psychiatry. He teaches Tai Chi Chuan, combining martial arts, somatics, and "streetwise medicine" at The Institute of Health and Healing, California Pacific Medical Center, San Francisco General Hospital's Diabetes Clinic, and The Integrative Center for Culture and Healing at St. Luke's Hospital (Sutter Health.) His organization, Beyond Anonymous, develops community-based recovery plans for people with any type of addictive problem.

taichisolutions@aol.com

Peter Reilly is director of the Lower Hudson Regional Information Center, a nonprofit consortium providing educational technology services to sixty-two school districts in three counties just north of New York City. Pete is a Master Somatic Coach and a former middle and high school English teacher. He lives with his wife Liz and their children Kate, Colleen, and Brian in Tomkins Cove, New York.

preilly@lhric.org

Judith Rosenberg is a social entrepreneur who has worked with low-income communities for the past thirty years. She develops peer support systems to enhance people's ability to work together, in the process starting grassroots nonprofit agencies and working within government systems. Her positions have ranged from social worker to strategic planner to executive director, in the Bay Area and Central America. Since 1991 she has served as the executive director of TEAMS: Transformation through Education and Mutual Support.

judithelise@cs.com

Karen Short, parent educator and Master Somatic Coach, is an active parent in her local school district. As a parent coach she works to restore harmony and mutual respect within families through using somatic and language techniques. Karen facilitates groups of parents to generate self-learning conversations, develop new practices, and build communities of parents who can restore the passion for successful parenting. She lives with her husband and two children in Santa Rosa, California.

K_Short@pacbell.net

Ariana Strozzi is cofounder of Strozzi Institute. Inspired by the demands of leadership she has faced in business and how they parallel in many ways her thirty-two years of working with animals, she created Leadership & Horses™ in 1990. This program integrates the discourses of business process, leadership, somatics, animal behavior, and horsemanship into a new metaphor for developing professional mastery, leadership, and team excellence. An avid businesswoman, artist, and horseman, she has trained horses for more than thirty-two years and has won championship awards in three-day eventing, jumping, dressage, western reining, and working cow horse.

www.leadershipandhorses.com

ariana@strozziinstitute.com

Richard Strozzi-Heckler, Ph.D., is an internationally known authority on leadership and mastery. In Search of the Warrior Spirit details the leadership program he developed for the United States Army Special Forces, which has become the foundation for his leadership programs in many different fields. His subsequent books have shown his approach to learning, mastery, and team building. He co-founded Strozzi Institute: The Center for Leadership and Mastery, as well as the Lomi School and Tamalpais Aikido Dojo. More recently in Petaluma he founded Two Rock Aikido Dojo. Richard holds a sixth-degree black belt in aikido as well as ranks in judo, jujitsu, and capoeira.

www.strozziinstitute.com

Mary Wagner's fiction has been awarded an O. Henry Award and a Pushcart Prize. She has taught creative writing at San Francisco State University and to prison parolees, and has taught self-defense to girls and women. In her teaching and coaching, she ensures that her clients harness the full potential of imagination, build the body and voice, the skills and practices, to fulfill their deepest aspirations. She is a Master Somatic Coach.

mmwagner@pacbell.net

Suzanne Zeman, MSC, brings thirty years of experience to her work as a somatic business coach. Her early careers as a research chemist and entrepreneur led her to coach managers, teams, and entrepreneurs in organizations ranging from nonprofits to Fortune 500 companies. She coaches managers and executives in Enterprise Performance's Mastering Professional Management program and is a senior associate at Strozzi Institute.

szeman@attbi.com

~ **Strozzi Institute** is an educational and research
organization that teaches leadership, personal,
and professional mastery skills to individuals as well as people
involved in the fields of business, education, health,
the military, and government.

For more information contact:

www.strozziinstitute.com

4101 Middle Two Rock Road, Petaluma, Ca. 94952

(707) 778-6505